Booker T's Child

The Life and Times of
Portia Marshall Washington Pittman

Portia, at piano.

Booker T's Child

The Life and Times of Portia Marshall Washington Pittman

by Roy L. Hill

Revised, Augmented Edition
Three Continents Press
3CP

©Roy L. Hill, Washington, D.C., 1993

Second Edition: Revised and Augmented
Three Continents Press
1901 Pennsylvania Avenue, N.W.
Washington, D.C. 20006

Library of Congress Cataloguing-in-Publication Data

Booker T's Child: the life and times of Portia Marshall
Washington Pittman / by Roy L. Hill. —Rev., augm. ed., 2nd ed.
    p.   cm.
Includes bibliographical references and index.
ISBN o-89410-748-8 (cloth) : $26.00. — ISBN 0-89410-749-6 (pbk)
: $15.00
    1. Pittman, Portia Marshall Washington, 1883-1978. 2. Afro
-Americans—Biography. 3. Afro-Americans—Civil rights.
4. Washington, Booker T., 1856-1915. 5. Music teachers—United
States—Biography. 6. Afro-Americans—Social conditions.
I. Title.
ML423.P57H54   1993   92-470-24
973.9'092—dc20   CIP
[B]   MN

ISBN: 0-89410-748-8 (cloth)
ISBN: 0-89410-749-6 (pbk)

Cover Art and all photographs (unless otherwise specified),
©Roy L. Hill, 1993.

This book is dedicated by
Portia Marshall Washington Pittman
to the memory of her father
Booker T. Washington
and by me
to her

To my very dear friend
Roye Hill,
    Mrs Marshall Washington Pittman
Please always remember — that I feel so close
to you as tho you were my own son — and I do
appreciate you — "Keep the Faith"

Kansas City Kan, June 15, '63 —

Portia's "Note" to Roy L. Hill.

ACKNOWLEDGEMENTS

There are so many whose names I would like to place here, for all of them have done so much to make possible my telling of Mrs. Pittman's story.

Before I became involved in this project, Mrs. Pittman was aided in assembling the recollectionf of her rich life by several people. Among these, I am most grateful to J. Vernon Brantley, whose efforts form a cornerstone of the present work.

I would like to thank also the following, without whose kindness my work could not have proceeded: Mrs. Fannie Howard Douglass, who was a constant inspiration in this project; Mrs. Nettie Washington Douglass, for her constant concern; Mrs. Edith Merriweather Washington, for the information she so unstintingly gave; Mrs. Nettie Hancock Washington, for the many questions she graciously found time to answer and Margaret Jane Washington Barrington, for information she supplied regarding John Henry Washington and his family.

In addition to these people and other members of the Washington family, my thanks are due to: Earl Howard, who served as Mrs. Pittman's secretary for a number of years; Dr. Vivien F. McBrier, for information on R. Nathaniel Dett; and Dr. Louis R. Harlan, for information derived from his years of Booker T. Washington research; Mrs. Phala Kennedy for all our discussions of

Margaret James Murray Washington; and Pauline W. Punch for various information she was able to give me on the Washington family; and Daniel T. Williams, Archivest of Tuskeege Institute Library.

There are others, too, without whom Portia's story could not have been told, and I want to express my gratitude to them here: Delores B. Reilly, Betty A. Williamson, and Lucille L. Bishop for their yeoman services in typing various stages of the manuscript; Roselie Stewart, of Hollywood, California, for her interest and support; and Susan F. Heimann, of New York, for her advice and assistance.

The author acknowledges his indebtedness to Dr. and Mrs. Frederick Doublass Patterson, President-Emeritus of Tuskegee Institute for additional advice and assistance; I am grateful to Dr. and Mrs. Luther H. Foster for their encouragement from the beginning to the completion of this biography.

Finally, I am greatly indebted to Dr. Eileen Jackson Southern of the Department of Afro-American Studies and Music, Harvard University, for invaluable criticism of its form and content. She is, of course, in no way responsible for the faults that remain.

CONTENTS

INTRODUCTION

On a day in September, 1946, I was at Washington, D.C.'s Union Station rushing to catch a train to my native South Carolina. Mrs. Portia Washington Pittman, the only daughter of Booker T. Washington, was also there that day, surrounded by a small crowd. I stopped and was introduced to Mrs. Pittman by Sidney J. Phillips, with whom she was working to have her father's birthplace made into a national shrine.

That brief meeting made no lasting impression on me. I was a young man, concerned principally with my education and with what kind of future I might have.

By 1958, when President Dwight D. Eisenhower sent troops into Little Rock, Arkansas, to integrate that city's Central High School, I had taught at Grambling College, Grambling, Louisiana; and Alcorn A. and M. College, Port Gibson, Mississippi; and was at Pennsylvania State University, University Park, Pennsylvania, working toward my doctorate in general speech. The problem of housing at Penn State was solved for my wife and me when Dr. Robert T. Oliver, the chairman of the speech department, provided quarters for us in his comfortable home. After breakfast one morning, Dr. Oliver and I had a conversatin about Booker T. Washington. In essence, he said he was sad about the decline of Washington's reputation among black people—particularly the young—and asked me my opinions on the subject. A few weeks later he suggested that I study Booker T. Washington for my course in American oratory.

I wrote to Edith M. Washington (Mrs. Ernest Davidson Washington), Washington's daughter-in-law, at Tuskegee Institute, for her suggestions. She replied saying, "The Booker T. Washington papers are in the manuscript room of the Library of Congress in Washington. You will find them most helpful. You might write to the Head Librarian at Tuskegee, Mr. M.D. Sprague. Hope you have success with your writing." Mrs. Washington also sent me Mrs. Pittman's address. That is how I came to renew my acquaintance with Mrs. Pittman in November, 1958. Thereafter, our lives began to overlap and finally seemed to synchronize. First, I was chosen as scriptwriter by a Hollywoood studio interested in doing a flim on Booker T. Washington. During my research for the script, I saw a lot of Mrs. Pittman and her son, Wiliam Sidney Pittman, and I also met Mrs. Nettie H. Washington (Mrs. Booker T. Washington, Jr.). When I was well into my writing, however, I was informed by the studio that Booker T. Washington, III had been selected to do the script instead. At about the same time, Mrs. Pittman started to talk about writing her memoirs and suggested that I work with her. In my natural disappointment about the film script, I did not warm up to the idea. But, in the ensuing years, Mrs. Pittman would call and write me occasionally, giving me descriptions of the progres of her memoirs toward publication—along with her often hilarious comments. Eventually, she managed to overcome my disinclination to the project, and I did become involved in helping Mrs. Pittman to tell her story.

That story is relevant in several areas. For the here and now it demonstrates that the best of hand-picked training and education, plus exposure to the white American and European cultures, did not eliminate from Mrs. Pittman's life or even alleviate any of the emotional stresses suffered by black Americans who did not have the experiences or opportunities she did. This tends to support the feeling of many of today's young blacks that rejection of black culture does not solve the human problems that are part of being black in a white society.

Historically, Mrs. Pittman's story offers a detailed picture— from a new point of view—of the private and public lives of Booker T. Washington, plus glimpses of the other actors (both black and white) on the world "stage" whose lives interacted with his.

Mrs. Pittman was a warm and intensely human being, whose life had not gone untouched by tragedy. Her story is also one of interaction, and thus her relationships to the other figures in the book are of paramount importance throughout—especially, of course, the one with her father. Clearly, some of the strongest threads in the skein of her life have their origins in that relationship. One of them is how she learned to survive being victimized by circumstances she was unable to control. The process began with her two stepmothers, one of whom strongly resented the child and started the apparent pattern of her youth—that of farming her out to live with various friends of the family. Perhaps even her years of study and travel in Europe—so easy to classify as part of her "education"—form part of that thread.

Even the largest-scale biography cannot offer every detail, even important ones. Here I would merely wish to comment that Portia's best friends were Hazel L. Harrison and Abby Mitchell, both musicians, who unnamed later in this work, must be remembered as warm supporters and fellow-artists during her often lonely days as a girl and young woman.

After I began to work with Mrs. Pittman, we naturally had many discussions about the title of her memoirs, and several ideas began to come together in my mind. First, it seemed to me from my research and interviews with her, members of the Washington family, and friends, that the young Mrs. Pittman had been out of the Washington home more than she had been in it. While her father traveled north in his fundraising efforts for Tuskegee, Mrs. Pittman was sent north and to Europe for her education. Then one day I found the old spiritual "Children, Go Where I Send Thee" echoing in my inner ear. Finally, it began to seem to me that in a sense we are all Booker T's children. We are all trying to attain something better, to "lift" ourselves, as he in his way came "up from slavery," moving from the life of a farmhand slave to white folks' kitchens to worldwide respect as one of the foremost educators of his time. It is practically a truism of life that in the attempt to rise above ourselves, no matter how hard we may try—and in what ways—every corner we turn seems to lead us straight back to ourselves. The essential lesson to be learned is that we must accept the past—though not, perhaps, uncritically—for whatever it has to teach us of grief, frustration, and guilt, and with whatever burdens of irredeemable obligation it may impose upon us. This is going where we are sent, for the sake of what it may help us to become.

Yes, Mrs. Pittman went where he sent her.

Yes, we are all Booker T's children, all going where we are sent and looking for avenues to move along. Perhaps in this way we will all learn to survive, to be functional in whatever walks of life we choose.

Mrs. Pittman learned survival and she learned more. She became good at languages because of her need to communicate her feelings, and very probably, her music was another function of that same need. While still a very young girl at Tuskegee, Mrs. Pittman heard the black pianist called Blind Tom (Thomas Greene Bethune, later known as Thomas Wiggins) and she found in music both a means of expression and a key that unlocked the door to an avenue of her own to move on. "It was Blind Tom who played a Liszt rhapsody that inspired me so early at Tuskegee. Until this day I have not forgotten that moment."

But that day or this, and whether she was at home or away, Mrs. Pittman's life has always been focused on one or the other. She often said to me in the course of our work together, "I want the world to get some real insight into my father's life. I want them to know that he was a real human being—he ate pigs-feet, drank liquor, and loved women. Some people say he ran after white women, but I never believed any of those stories."

For his child, Booker T. Washington is still the center of the world, and perhaps two episodes that I shared with Mrs. Pittman in her eighty-seventh year will make clear how strong an influence that "center" exerted on her.

In April, 1970, I drove from Washington to Tuskegee with Mrs. Pittman and her daughter Fannie Virginia for the celebration of Founders Day. At Tuskegee I met Edith Johnston Clark, Booker T. Washington's grand-niece; and his niece, Margaret Washington Barrington.

Later, when Phala Kennedy, the wife of the late Dr. J. A. Kennedy of Tuskegee, entertained us in her home, the conversation turned to "Uncle Booker" and "Aunt Maggie" Washington. (Mrs. Kennedy had grown up in the home of the third Mrs. Washington, and related several interesting anecdotes from that experience to me.) Talking about Mrs. Pittman's marriage, Mrs.

Barrington said, "The first time I saw Uncle Booker cry was when he gave you away at your wedding. After a brief exchange about whether the ceremony had taken place in the Oaks (the Washington home at Tuskegee) or in the domed dining room of the Institute itself, Mrs. Pittman said, "Anyway, I glanced at my stepmother Maggie and, you know, she beamed when he offered my hand." As I listened to this discussion of events more than half a century past, my mind was full of questions. Mrs. Pittman seemed to sense at least one of them, for she turned to me and said—with a small smile—"My stepmother must have thought, 'Now you are out of the way and I have your father to myself'."

But no matter how important long-ago people and events may be to her, the past is not where Mrs. Pittman lives, and she often speaks of her desire to share life and experiences with young people. On July 8, 1970, she came to the Newark campus of Rutgers to spend the day talking with some of my students (who were admittedly mainly interested in her memories of her father). The warm give-and take of that day was her way of reaching out across a gap of more than four generations, into today's very different world.

Mrs. Pittman said that her father's non-violent approach and his ideas of racial cooperation were all part of his dedication to humanity as a whole. When she was asked about the different approach of her father's contemporary W.E.B. DuBois, she commented that it had been Washington who first introduced DuBois to the public, as well as the poet Paul Laurence Dunbar. As a New Englander, she explained, DuBois had judged black people along the same lines at the whites he knew. "He never saw the poverty and ignorance of the Negro people after slavery," she said. "After he taught in the South a few years, though, he admitted that my father was right." (In an aside, she also added that DuBois had been "the type of man a woman would love.") To the question of whether she thought her father's or DuBois' philosophy would be most applicable to the current situation, she replied only that she thought it as was "good the Lord took (Washington) before all this happened. It would have confused him."

Mrs. Pittman remembered her father as a diplomat who often found himself caught between whites and blacks. "Theodore Roosevelt never made a move in the South without consulting my father"—and if this produced envy, resentment, or outright

xv

opposition in some sectors of both races, his "sincerity and humility were the reasons for the great respect many people gave him." She also recalled his good relationships with Presidents Taft and McKinley, "but not with Woodrow."

She went on to say that she didn't know what her father's reaction to the Black Panthers, Malcolm X, and other militant or activist black groups and leaders would be, describing militancy as "so out of his line" and commenting that "we don't get anything by being too violent." In a seeming volte-face, however, after mentioning her admiration for the late Dr. Martin Luther King, Jr., she said it was "natural" for people to have revolutions and added that if she were in school, she would be with the rebels, "but not the most militant ones." She stressed again that her father's goal had been to "lift, lift, lift," and stated that she agreed with him in regarding education as the best means by which that lifting could be accomplished. She said, "I was educated in New England and Europe, in the best schools. I taught at Booker T. Washington High School in Dallas, Texas, and at Tuskegee. I gave concerts in New York and Washington to help talented young musicians go to Europe for further study. Oh, maybe I wasn't as good as the reviews said. I really think that people wanted to see and hear Booker T. Washington's child."

This is her story.

Roy L. Hill
Rutgers—The State University
Newark, New Jersey
September, 1973

ONE

"Ain't every day we party with Booker T's child
and that child is for real."

On her 86th birthday, June 6, 1969, Mrs. Pittman was scheduled to be interviewed on one of Washington's T.V. stations. The appearance had to be cancelled, however, because of an unexpected gift from her then-current "beau." This 67-year old gentleman, unmindful of the of the historical importance of the day and of Booker T's child, had presented her with her first black eye. "Some gift," said Mrs. Pittman of this inappropriate birthday present, "but that's life. I guess a little love tap now and then makes the world go round." Then she added, "I still prefer the long-stemmed roses Duke Ellington sent me."

For her 87th birthday, Mrs. Pittman decided to have a week-long celebrations, involving people from all sides of her many faceted life—those of the so-called high and middle class, and those she has described as having "no class at all."

She recalls that birthday now with mixed emotions. "Child, I was so happy I felt like I was planning my debut or something. At 87, most people are planning their funerals, you know." The note of laughter in her voice disappears, however, as she adds, "I didn't get any newspaper coverage at all. My beginners and the second and third year students were pretty good." But her quick laugh returns soon. "Honey, after the way those fourth year students messed up, I was kind of glad there was no publicity."

1

The schedule she had devised for her six-day gala was a full one. On June 1, there was a recital by her beginning music students, and each of the next three days saw performances by her second, third, and fourth year pupils. The refreshments included punch; that creamy confection of custard, cake, fruit, and jam known as trifle; and German chocolate cake—the recipe given her by her landlady in her own long-ago days as a music student in Berlin.

The plans for June 5 were different. That evening there was a dinner for some of Mrs. Pittman's students, their parents, and a few friends. During the cocktails before the meal, she raised her glass in an anticipatory toast to herself, declaring "Tomorrow will be my glorious day."

Two days later, in tones that were understandably somewhat weary, she asked me a few questions about that day, starting with, "Was I really at my all-night party or did I just black out?" I replied that I would find it hard to paint a true word-picture of what had gone on, on June 6, and added, "Really, Mrs. Pittman, I think a line from Dunbar would just about sum it up" 'An' dey ain't no use in talkin', we jes- had one scrumptious time.'" I told her it had indeed been an all-night party, and that I assumed the drinks consumed had "preserved" the guests and so had played a part in making the party last as long as it did. But Mrs. Pittman wanted to know more. "Were you there? What really went on?"

You played the piano," I said. "You talked about Blind Tom and Blind Lemon Jefferson, too, and all the days gone by. You had a fine time. I took all the calls and messages and tried to be cool. Big Maybelle called to say she couldn't drink anymore, but her thoughts were with you. Sara Lou Longview made you a toast: 'Live, live, live; love, love, love; run fast; carry on for days; and don't lose a thing in real life." Your friend Living Good Franklin called from Dallas. Pee Wee, Kingfish, Edna, Greta, and Paula all wished you a Happy Birthday, but either they were drunk on corn liquor or there's lot of laryngitis going around, 'cause they were kind of hard to understand on the phone. Oh, yes, and several of the old stars came by."

"You know," Mrs. Pittman interrupted me, "the old stars come up slow and last forever. The new ones come up like a fire and pass so swiftly, like the flame. Life is like that. It comes and then it goes. I guess it's like this room full of flowers—beautiful for a while and then they pass on.

Then I had to continue my recital.

"Aunt Lizzie smoked her corn pipe and gave us a reading of a Langston Hughes' poem "The Negro Mother." Baby Ray and Bobby Doll sang what they said was your favorite song, 'I'll Be Around," and talked about your brothers Booker and Dave. Mattiwilda Voorhees tried to sing 'Bless This House' after she conducted 'Happy Birthday." Hazel and Martha Jean started the Charles L. Johnson and Dora Dean cakewalk of 1895."

We had to stop there as Mrs. Pittman asked, "Which one was Charles?" and I replied that I hadn't been able to tell.

There was a lot more party to remember, for after all it had only really gotten underway at about midnight when Ted Goodall, a neighbor, stepped through the door all decked out in pea-green pants in honor of Mrs. Pittman's great day. He was carrying a plate of fried chicken that was almost as hot as he was (Ted was steaming because an old friend had just walked out on him). The familiar face of Cora, the late Sidney Pittman's girlfriend, could be seen in the crowd. Cora was wearing black but she seemed happy to be part of this occasion and to be with her almost-in-laws once more.

Mamie, Lois, Rachel, Leelu, Pearl, Carrie Long, Dee, Irma Lou Lee, Eddie Lee, Paul, and Jay were among the guests. Lois ate so much she was sick. Rachel told jokes and laughed and did her famous belly roll, though she, too, said she had a stomach-ache. Paul had a black book that could have been the Bible. Fannie Virginia accompanied Pearl on the piano while she sang "Ain't Misbehavin'." Then Andy took over and played "Milk Cow Blues." At that point, the janitor came upstairs from his basement apartment to complain about the noise and hush everyone down, but then he stayed to join us and make some noise of his own.

Once Mrs. Pittman raised her voice, happy if a little woozy, to inquire, "Did anyone thank the good Lord for what we are about to receive?" "No, ma'am," Paul said, "there ain't no preacher here tonight." Paraphrasing a line from Dunbar, Mrs. Pittman went on, "Where's the 'possum and sweet potatoes?" Mamie, thinking she was serious, began to enumerate: "We had chicken Mister Teddie cooked and brought, cornbread and peas, Cora brought pig feet, hog ears, and chitlin's I brought—some people call them Kansas City Wranglers—Roy Lee brought the corn whiskey, beer, and gin,

3

and somebody else brought the ice."

Elaine, Ruth and Hortense sat and observed like queens at a command performance while Vivian and Frances played the piano and sang "I Like Cake and No Mistake," which seemed to be a signal for something-or-other. When the cake was in Oliver and Eileen wanted to cut it German-style.

Mary Lou arrived next, saying she wanted to meet the man who was writing *Booker T's Child*. She was all dressed in white— white shoes, white stockings, white hat, white dress—and carrying a white pocketbook that we knew contained the numbers for tomorrow.

During a brief lull, Leelu yelled out, "Let's get on with the party. This isn't the Canterbury Tales, it's Portia's eighty-seventh party, not her seventh!" There was more singing, and more drinking, and through it all echoes of conversation reached me like sunrays breaking through patches of fog.

"You know, Mrs. Pittman lives in the past."

"And what a glorious, historical past it must be. She's romantic history."

"No, honey, she's ancient history."

Finally, at 5 A.M., Mrs. Pittman in her black lace dress stood in the doorway at the top of the steps, kissing and shaking hands with her guests as they left. She claimed that part of the reason she felt so young was her dislike for having anything "old" around her. "What a party it has been," she said over and over.

There would be—and had been—other parties and occasions of which she might be moved to comment, "Those melodious moments of which friends are composed," and there would be— and had been—other birthdays for Portia Marshall Washington Pittman.

One that she remembers well as celebrated in 1901 at Tuskegee. That day was a Sunday, and so it began like other Sundays, with services in the chapel. A magnificent building for its day— some 110 feet long, with a seating capacity of 2400, a large minister's study, and steam heat—it was her father's pride and joy.

Mrs. Pittman remembers how the yellow pine-oak floors gleamed in the morning light streaming in through the windows. "Poppa, the chapel is so beautiful," she said. Booker T. smiled, "Yes, but it's more than just beautiful. There are almost

4

150,000,000 bricks in that building. Every brick in it, save one, was made on the campus by students of the Institute, and was laid by students. The architect was a colored member of the faculty, Robert R. Taylor, a graduate of Massachusetts Institute of Technology. The one brick that was not made at Tuskegee Institute came from the little cabin in Malden in West Virginia in which the boy, Booker T. Washington, first began to dream of education for himself and then for his race. And as generation after generation of eager youth assemble in that chapel, and gaze at those windows, their hopes and ambitions are linked with the suffering and struggles of their forefathers and with the destiny of their race as it rises to play its part in the whole community of mankind, as seen by them in the context of loyalty to the Christian meaning of life.

TWO

The quality of mercy is not strain'd;
It droppeth as the gentle rain from heaven
Upon the place beneath. It is twice blest—
It blesseth him that gives and him that takes.
'Tis mightiest in the mightiest. It becomes
The throned monarch better than his crown.
His sceptre shows the force of temporal power,
The attribute to awe and majesty,
Wherein doth sit the dread and fear of kings;
But mercy is above this sceptred sway;
It is enthroned in the hearts of kings,
It is an attribute of God himself;
And earthly power doth then show likest God's
When mercy seasons justice.

Merchant of Venice Act IV, Scene I, II. 184-197

There had not always been a chapel at Tuskegee, and during the early years, Sunday morning services were held in a room set aside for the purpose in Porter Hall, the school's first building, and before that, wherever they could be accommodated. The completion, in 1896, of the building—which took two years to construct and most of the money for which was donated by the late Caroline and Olivia E. Phelps Stokes of New York—marked a kind of watershed. Before, it could be said that the school had been engaged as much in a struggle for its very existence as in the business of education.

And there had not always been the easy companionship and sense of communication between herself and her father that Portia remembers from the morning of her eighteenth birthday—for, from Booker T's side at least, there simply had not been time. Still, an almost negative way, the story of Portia's first eighteen years parallels—and is intricately entwined with—that of the school to which her father devoted his whole life and energeis with such single-minded purpose.

Portia was born June 6, 1883, barely two years after her father—a graduate of Virginia's Hampton Institute (itself founded only in 1868)—had started Tuskegee with little more than a tumbledown shack next to the town's black Methodist church and his own inordinate will to work. By 1881, the school's original enrollment of thirty students had more than tripled, and four teachers—two men and two women—were helping Booker T. to attain his goal. In that time, too, as might any young man who had begun to make his way up in his chosen field, he started to think in terms of having a real home of his own—and of a wife to make that home for him.

He had first met Fannie Norton Smith in Malden, West Virginia. Malden was where his mother and stepfather had gone with the 10-year-old Booker and his half-brother and -sister after the Emancipation Proclamation was read from the front of the Burroughs farm (too small to be considered a real Southern plantation, even by post-Civil War standards), where he had been a slave. And Malden was where he returned after his graduation from Hampton to take up his first job as a teacher.

Fannie, like her husband, had graduated from Hampton (in 1882). After the wedding, they returned almost immediately to Tuskegee. In *Up From Slavery*, Booker T. describes Fannie's "earnest and constant work in the interests of the school" and speaks of how, "from the first (she) earnestly devoted her thoughts and time to the work of the school and was completely one with me

7

in every interest and ambition. She passed away, however, before she had an opportunity of seeing what the school was designed to be." Just before this passage, the single sentence appears: "One child, Portia M. Washington, was born during our marriage."

But if these paragraphs are so terse as to verge on the laconic, and if wife and child seem most definitely to take second place to Tuskegee, there is still in their very brevity a flavor about them of a recollection of gentler days that are gone—no matter what hardships may have been involved. What Portia has to say about those days bears this out:

"My mother was a childhood sweetheart of Booker's from the early Malden days. While teaching there, he trained her in preparation for Hampton Institute. When he taught at Hampton himself, she was a student there and their love deepened. He came down to Tuskegee in 1881 to start the school and then returned to Hampton the year she graduated to marry her and bring her back to Tuskegee. The marriage was on August 12, 1882, in Tahter Rice's Zion Baptist Church in Tinkersville, West Virginia. They began housekeeping that early fall, at Tuskegee, and their home gave the four teachers at the school a home, too. My mother is supposed to have had Indian blood—she was light brown and had high cheekbones, so she must have looked it.

"I was born June 6, 1883, and I was the first child born on the Tuskegee campus. The physician who performed the delivery was Doctor W.J. Gautier of Tuskegee. He was French, I believe, or he certainly had a French name.

"About my names: my father read the plays of Shakespeare every day, and he really loved *Merchant of Venice*. I was named Portia for the character in it he admired the most—you know the famous speech she makes about mercy. My middle name comes about because of General James Fowler Baldwin Marshall. The General was treasurer of Hampton while my father studied there and helped him a lot—both then and later, after the beginning of Tuskegee.

"I think it's important to mention that my parents were very happy together, but it only lasted such a brief time. My mother was just a girl when she died—so young—26 years old. That was in May, 1884. So I know what the loss of a mother is like, though I can't really say that I remember her.

"I have heard people say, though, that she was a great inspiration to my father and that he loved her dearly. Fifty years later the old citizens of Tuskegee would still speak of her as kind, modest, and mingling helpfully with the people of the town, and eager to carry forward my father's work whenever he was away in those early days.

"They said that my father almost lost his mind when she died—that we were going to lose him, too. In that time he couldn't sleep, you know, and he would just get up and walk and walk, up and down the road. This would go on long and far into the night. He was just absolutely torn to pieces by her death.

"But she was as unobtrusive in her death as she had been in life, and even its cause is uncertain. A local newspaper reported it as 'consumption of the bowels.' But according to our family tradition, it was due to internal injuries. It seems there was some kind of picnic, and she was riding in a farm wagon and fell out. This was shortly after I was born. Anyway, they didn't have surgery in those days, and she didn't recover, and it was many months that she had to ride in a wheel chair.

"The loss to my father was terrible, and his grief was tremendous. Such a young man, just starting out with his wife, and hoping to have a large family and only one gal born.

"Yes, I really know what the loss of a mother is like.

"Almost every time that my Aunt Mandy—we were always being told not to call her that but to use her full name, Amanda—came to Tuskegee, she would cry because she was so proud of her brother. Whenever I asked her what she was crying for, she'd say, "Just think what a little slave boy has accomplished."

" But my father never really experienced the harshest forms of slavery, you know. My maternal grandmother, Jane Burroughs, was a house slave, and so was he, most of the time. That meant they had higher status and a lighter work load and better food than real field slaves. Sometimes house servents even began to think like the master and his family—to identify with them, you might say. In any case, my father was five when his master died, and freedom came four years later.

"My father was born on that farm, at Hale's Ford, in Franklin County, Virginia. That's in the western part of the state, about 16 miles south of Roanoke. His mother was a cook and one of the ten

9

slaves they owned there. He had blue eyes, which was because his father was a white man. It may have been someone named Hatcher, but no one is certain. There was a Hatcher family in the neighborhood, but in those days you can be sure they wouldn't have admitted to such a thing, even though it went on all the time under slavery. My Uncle John's father was a white man, too, who was said to be in the army John and my father were both born before my grandmother married Washington Ferguson, the slave of a neighboring farmer. Amanda was their daughter, and she was darker than either of her half brothers. Now the place where they were born is a national memorial, because of my father; I did a lot of the work toward making that possible."

THREE

"To have had a Mother...how mighty."

"My mother knew that she was going to die. She suggested several times that my father replace her with Miss Olivia A. Davidson."

And so the gentle Fannie was gone, leaving behind a grief-stricken husband of 28 and an 11-month-old baby, of whom a friend later wrote that she was "left to sustain with her father a loss which she can never know." For the young widower, this was a time of monstrously ballooning problems that soon threatened to overwhelm him, and what could be more natural than for the troubled Booker T. to look to family, to roots, for help? Portia says he did so:

"In my father's loneliness and his need for a feminine hand in caring for me, he turned to old friends. My grandmother, Celia Norton Smith, came down to Tuskegee for a visit. She had never been enthusiastic about her daughter's marriage so far from home, to a young man who had not yet made his way in the world. My mother's early death seemed to confirm her judgement, and when she arrived at Tuskegee she was in a mood to scold my father for whatever real or fancied neglect had caused her daughter's death.

11

Then the Alabama climate didn't agree with her, and she was homesick for West Virginia, so she just didn't like anything at Tuskegee.

"One day my grandmother simply stole me. She got on a train at Chehaw Station and left for Malden. That was the way I had my first train ride. Of course I was too young at the time to remember it, but train rides would always make me sick later on, when I was a girl. Do you know, my father had to get the police to help bring me back home again?"

While he was thus occupied, time was at work too, slowly and almost imperceptibly deadening the pain of Booker T's loss, and so it in no way detracts from his feeling for Fannie that he married again in 1885, less than a year after her death. There were Tuskegee and his infant daughter to think about. He still needed help with what were now his two prime considerations in life.

The woman he chose had been involved in the first of those concerns almost as long as he had himself. And in *Up From Slavery* he writes of her that "at the end of the first six weeks, a new and rare face entered the school as a co-teacher." Olivia A. Davidson was also possessed of a rare determination and a will to succeed in life that equaled her future husband's.

Born in 1854 (she was about two years older than Booker T.), she may had been one of the fifteen slaves reported in 1860 by James C. Davidson of Tazewell County, Virginia. Her mother, Eliza Davidson, went north after the war—possibly with homeward-bound Union troops, because she was said to have been a servant of General George Armstrong Custer's—and settled with her large family of children in the small village of Albany, in Athens County, Ohio. There, black effort plus a small grant from a white philanthropist had combined to establish an excellent black private school called the Albany Enterprise Academy. After her graduation from the school, Olivia, her brother Joseph, and a sister or sister-in-law travelled into the Deep South to teach freedmen in Hernando, Mississippi.

But during this period, which Booker T. described as "the darkest part of the Reconstruction days," the Ku Klux Klan was operating throughout the South (and elsewhere as well). In one of its nightime raids in the Hernando area, Olivia's two relatives became some of the "not a few coloured people (who) lost their lives."

12

Olivia then moved to Memphis, Tennessee, to continue her teaching career. In 1878, however, while she was at home in Ohio during her vacation, yellow fever struck in Memphis. The outbreak rapidly reached epidemic proportions, and eventually claimed more than 4,000 victims. Olivia telegraphed the Memphis mayor her offer to serve as a nurse, but since she had not been immunized against the disease, he insisted she stay away until the epidemic was over. In this indirect fashion, she set foot on the path that lead to her meeting Booker T.

Now Olivia enrolled at Hampton, and was found so well prepared that she was placed in the senior class. (Mrs. Rutherford B. Hayes—the first lady whose teetotaling serving habits in the White House had earned her the not entirely flattering sobriquet "Lemonade Lucy"—had established the scholarship which enabled her to attend.) Olivia's academic abilities impressed everyone at Hampton, as did her grace, tact, and maturity. Her qualities also attracted the attention of a wealthy Hampton donor, Mrs. Mary Tilesteon Hemenway of Boston.

Mrs. Hemenway paid the expenses for Olivia's two-year course at Framingham State Normal School near Boston, another recipient of her philanthropies. Though she was fair enough to pass for white among the Northern strangers, Olivia always maintained that she was proud to be a Negro. She excelled in her work in New England, too, and made friends who were later to be of help to Tuskegee. She acquired in addition a sophistication in teaching techniques that Booker T.—for all his self-assurance—could not match.

He had decided only three days after he opened Tuskegee on July 4, 1891, that some assistance was required, and after Olivia's arrival, the two worked side by side, sharing both the burdens and the vision of what the future held for the school. Olivia's special forte was persuading the girl students, fresh from the tenant shacks of the Black Belt South, to emulate the genteel sensibility, feminine modesty, and the New England self-restraint she had learned in her days at Framingham.

Booker T. also found much to comment in Olivia, and—tellingly, perhaps—almost immediately began to describe their on-going work at Tuskegee in terms of "we": "Miss Davidson and I began consulting as to the future of the school from the first," he says, and goes on to describe the difficulties inherent in teaching

13

the students more than mere "book learning." There was the problem of changing their whole life-style, which was infinitely larger than that of simply imparting knowledge. It was the attitudes of the constantly arriving students that required the most work. "There was a desperate need to teach them...how to care for their bodies. We wanted to teach them what to eat, and how to eat it properly, and how to care for their rooms....We wanted to teach them to study actual things instead of mere books alone."

This was a task so large and time-consuming that it needed all of Booker T's attention. He would "spring up on" some department or another, checking unexpectedly on their progress, and it must have been at this early date that he formed a habit Portia recalls:

I remember his getting up in the morning, sometimes when it was real cold and he wouldn't take time to put on all of his clothing, but he had a big overcoat and would slip that over his nightclothes and ride down to the students' dining room...to see if their meals were properly prepared. He also would see if they were waiting on tables correctly, and if they were doing it in an orderly way.

Booker T. and Olivia continued their work as man and wife, and Portia acquired a stepmother when she was two years old.

FOUR

"I was a serious child."

Which of us has not, as an adult, experienced that strange coming face-to-face with things in the "real" world which are nothing like we remember them to be? The hayloft on the farm has lost the soaring heights of Everest. The huge, threatening dog— long dead now—who guarded the house on the corner with his wolflike fangs and visious snarls—was just a small, ill-tempered mongrel. And the boy or girl next door, who loomed so large in all of our adolescent plans, is no more than another ordinary human being. Everything is smaller, less intense. All the proportions have changed radically.

Have our memories been deceiving us? Do photographs lie? Where is the truth?

The fact is that for most of us there are many truths, each valid for its own time; and that experience can alter truth—and vice-versa. While it reaches toward some sort of synthesis within us, it colors and shapes what we remember, as the people who once were color and shape who we are today. But neither necessarily calls the other into question.

It is an equally human reaction to remember events and assign them reasons much, much later. Psychologists tell us that young children often equate the death of a parent—especially that of a mother who has been the center of their world until then—with a desertion of themselves. It is not always true, as one nineteenth-

15

century children's author believed, that because a child's mother..."died when she was born...she had never known or missed her." A real mother, perhaps particularly one who *is* unknown and therefore only heard about, leaves a tailor-made void waiting to be filled. To refer again to children's literature, "wicked stepmothers" have been favorite ogre figures since long before Cinderella.

When her father married Olivia Davidson on August 11, 1885, Portia was just at that age at which a child's consciousness of its surroundings, and most importantly, of other people, begins to find expression. Her memories of this period in her life are tempered by a striving to be fair:

"I wonder if that is the reason I used to be so afraid of the dark. I guess a child without a mother will grow up like that. My father's second wife was a very different type of girl. She was a very fine and honest woman, but very firm, and she certainly had her own ideas about everything.

"One of those things was my fear of the dark. Sometimes she would make me stand out of doors after dark because she thought that was a good way to make me get over it. She had known my real mother for years, and they had been great friends, and so she felt that it was her duty to look after me in that way."

And that is what the no-nonsense Olivia continued to do, applying her "rare moral character and...unselfishness" equally to Portia and to Tuskegee. Whatever her effect on them, on Booker T. ... she was a good influence. The emotional depression that had gripped him following Fannie's death began to lift and dissipate. He even lost a little of that brusque, full-of-business air that was formerly so characteristic of him. And then, on May 29, 1887, at Boston's New England General Hospital, Booker T. and Olivia's first child was born—a boy who was named Booker Taliaferro Washington, Junior.

Portia's father was the kind of man to whom a son to carry on his name and possibly his work meant a great deal, and his pride shines through in *Up From Slavery* (in striking contrast to the earlier, austere almost-footnote about his daughter). The unaccustomed word "love" began to appear in his letters home—for, soon after the birth of his son, Booker T. was again ringing Northern doorbells, seeking contributions for Tuskegee.

Portia called the new baby simply Brother, a nick-name that stuck and became the family's pet name for him. Two years later, Olivia rounded out the Washington family by presenting her husband with the second of what he was to call his "two bright, beautiful boys," Ernest Davidson Washington. This little boy was later known as Dave.

But Booker T's horizon was not completely unclouded, for Olivia was not well. The work as Tuskegee's "Lady Principal" had taken a heavy toll of her energies, and she had never been as strong as she seemed. Portia remembers:

"I have been told that my mother Olivia had a mysterious physical weakness. She had collapsed in 1881, after graduation from Framingham, and she collapsed again the summer of 1884. She entered a Boston hospital, where doctors were unsuccessful in discovering the nature of her illness. They didn't know if it was her mind, her nerves, some internal physical disorder, or just over-work. They didn't know and she didn't. Her old friend Mrs. Mary Hemenway came to visit her almost daily and offered to help her in any way she needed. But my mother Olivia just couldn't bring herself to ask for any more from the kind old woman. She spent a short time with a former Framingham classmate, and then went up to Spruce Cottage, in Jackson, New Hampshire, to rest for the summer. That was before she married my father."

At this time, Olivia wrote wistfully to an old friend, "I think I would never grow tired and sick if I could when at work drop all now and then." She thought of returning to the hospital for more tests, but as she regained her strength, she began to feel somehow guilty for having become ill at all. In the fall she returned to her post at Tuskegee, and to her future husband.

At Tuskegee, on February 8, 1889, while Olivia was still recuperating from the difficult birth of her second son, a defect in a chimney caused a fire to break out. Portia tells it this way:

"I remember we had a big fireplace in one of the rooms. Something was the matter with it, because it made the roof catch fire. This was shortly after the birth of my youngest brother. My mother Olivia was lying in bed, and they brought her out on a mattress and put her in the yard. I remember someone yelling "Where's the baby!" and then they took the baby out. Everyone was every confused.

"I was in bed somewhere in the house, and they said, 'Don't forget the little girl,' and the next thing was someone was taking me out. This was all after four in the morning, and it was a bitter cold night. I think I was saved by the woman who was nursing me. She took care of us through all the day, and we kept her with us for years and years. I will never forget her—also because she was the first person I knew who came from Nostasulga. That name must have impressed me as a child. Anyway, my mother Olivia's health never did get straight again; she was all sort of shaken up afterwards and she never got her strength back.

"My father moved her to Massachusetts General Hospital in Boston, and she lingered for three months. You know, whenever she gained consciousness my father was there, but whatever he tried to do was no good."

Olivia died on May 9, 1889. Once more, the responsibility of Tuskegee was his to carry alone. This time, in additions, he had three children—the boys, aged two years and six months, and the six-year-old Portia:

"So my father had great tragedy in his life. He had so many things happen to him that if he hadn't been a very dedicated person, I think he would have given it up. But he was a rugged character who had to do what he was sent here to do.

"He would personally pick his teachers. He would go out to all the different schools and get the finest teachers he could, who had graduated from Harvard, Yale, Fisk, and places like that. He would find out for himself if they were suited to teach at Tuskegee. Going to Alabama was quite a sacrifice at that time, you know. It was nothing like it is now.

"And it was very hard for him after my mother Olivia died, when he had to care for three small children all alone. I remember that we lived in a two-story frame house then, on the campus. I was stricken with thyphoid fever. Our chaplain's wife took care of me— she was from Atlanta, Georga—such a lovely woman and just like a mother to me. I'll never forget her for that. I was so sick and had such a fever that they had to send for ice for me, every day. It would have to come all the way from Montgomery on a freight train. There was no other way to get the ice to Tuskegee, but they never failed as I can recall.

"As busy as he was, my father would look after me, too. I remember that we used to be bothered with bedbugs, then—that's something I'm not ashamed to tell. I can remember my father getting up real early one morning to take out our mattresses and spray them with kerosene to kill the bugs. That's something you might never have heard of anyone doing unless you lived then. Another thing I also remember is those big old tin tubs that servants and mothers used to wash your clothes in."

FIVE

"Sometimes I feel like a motherless child."

All of the physical needs of the three motherless Washington children—the youngest members of what people were already beginning to consider the "royal family" of Tuskegee—were indeed being seen to, but now there were only servants to wash their clothes. For Portia, especially, this meant that not only was there no real mother to provide her with the loving emotional support so essential to any child, but there was no longer even the firm guidance that Olivia had begun to supply. Much of the everyday work of caring for the children was done by Portia's Uncle John and by Aunt Susie, his wife. There was also a succession of women and girls who were hired as nursemaids.

Some comfort, however, came from Olivia's family in Ohio—especially from her sister, Mary Elliott, who ran a millinery shop in Columbus. Shortly after Olivia's death, she wrote to Portia, though the little girl was not really a relative at all: "We are all proud of (Davidson's) name; how I would like to see him, and all of you, my darling little children, and take you in my arms and kiss you over and over again," she wrote, marking some kisses on the page. The letter continues, "You have got a grandma Davidson, up in this county where I live, that talks a great deal about you children. She wants to see you so badly. She is getting to be old and she can't see you unless you come to see me and then she will get on the train and come to my house to see you. She has seen yours and Brother's picture."

Mrs. Elliott's words are an attempt to convey a sense of family, of belonging, that was all too lacking from life at Tuskegee and that she must have known Booker T. was incapable of giving. As always, he was away in the North for long periods of time. The letter is significant for another reason—it was addressed to Portia, and she was the only one of the three children who was old enough to read and thus old enough to go to school.

There had not yet been enough time for Portia to develop much feeling of any kind toward her two small half-brothers—not even natural sibling rivalry or the jealousy of the eldest toward the younger ones that might have been expected. She says now of Booker T. that his "forward-looking care"—a blend of "affection" and "direction"—did not combine well with a life that was "so systematic and full of work that he had little to say to his children." The same combination may well have influenced him in his choice of a New England country school far away from home for what was still only a very young child. But Portia adds, "He wanted me to have the very best training possible."

En route to starting that training, the much-desired visit with Mary Elliott, the aging Eliza, and the other Davidsons finally took place. Mrs. Dora S. King of Hanover, Massachusetts, who was hired as a nurse in the early summer of 1890, picked up the children at Tuskegee and brought them to her home town, travelling by way of Ohio. The almost proprietary interest of the Davidson relatives in Booker T's children continued after that, and Olivia's brother Hiram—an employee of the state mental institution in Columbus—wrote to his brother-in-law expressing his approval of Mrs. King's abilities as a nurse and of how she was handling the children, calling her a "model both intellectually and morally."

Mrs. King also kept Booker T. posted on his children's progress, sending him periodic reports—and questions. She obviously had the children and the welfare of their developing personalities very much at heart. As a Northerner, she found some of their customs "distinctly southern," and, it would seem, not completely to her liking. Among these was the fact that Portia was being called "sister" and Booker "brother" not only by family but by outsiders as well. "Do you wish Portia and Baker to call Davidson brother?" she inquired of her father. "You may or may not know that Baker seriously objects to being called brother. I have often heard him tell the teachers at Tuskegee that his name was not brother but Baker." It is at least a reasonable assumption that Booker T. did not know, and his reaction—if any—to Mrs. King's rather prim letter has not survived. In any case, the wishes of the assertive three-year-old did prevail, and it was as Baker that he was known until he reached adulthood.

The children spent the summer in Hanover, arriving on June 12 and boarding there with a Mrs. Winslow. Most of Portia's memories of the period are vague and made up only of the sort of thing that might stick in any impressionable child's mind: "Once I saw a snake in the road on the way to school." Another thing that has stayed with her is what she calls "my first experience of being the only colored girl in the school," which caused her the painful feeling of being alone and different.

It was a short experience—since Mrs. King returned the children to Tuskegee in the fall—but it is one that she was to repeat throughout her life, as was that of missing her father. A letter of Portia's probably enclosed with one of Mrs. King's notes, tells the story: "I have been going to school four days now. The first day I was homesick, but I am not now. I am having a good time every day. I am getting real fat." A short, childish note, and it says something for Booker T. that it was saved, but like another of Shakespeare's women, the lady did "protest too much"—if only with the simple words at her command. Was her father, too, aware of its plaintive tone?

Whether he was or was not, circumstances were soon to produce a changed situation.

A month after Olivia's death, Booker T. had attended the graduation ceremonies at Fisk University, in Nashville, Tennessee. The school, founded in 1865, with a racially mixed faculty and a black student body, prided itself on its resemblance to Ohio's Oberlin College and to Hampton Institute. During his stay at Fisk, which had provided him with good teachers in the past, he met a 24-year old member of the senior class, named Margaret James Murray. She had already written to him about the possibilities of her working at Tuskegee and now, struck by her poise, personality, and sharp wit, Booker T. hired her to teach English. A year later, she was to become the school's Lady-Principal, as Olivia had been before her.

Like Olivia, too, Margaret was very light-skinned. Her father had been a white man, but she told conflicting stories about him. In one version, he was James Murray, an Irishman onto whose name she tacked an "Esq.," thus glamorizing him almost as other blacks, coming fresh—and nameless—from slavery, glamorized themselves by taking on what they called their "entitles." Later, she amended the tale, saying her father was from Macon, Mississippi. Her mother's background was a simpler one, or it was certainly more difficult to obscure—she was a black, Georgia-born washerwoman named Lucy Murray.

Whatever her origins, Margaret's father had died when she was seven, leaving her one small member of an extremely poor family of ten. By a stroke of luck her early education was provided by a Quaker brother-and-sister teaching team in Macon, and she did so well with them that she soon decided to follow in their footsteps and become a teacher herself. In her six years at Fisk—where she took what today would be considered a liberal arts program, including courses in Latin, Greek, German, French, philosophy, literature, and science—Margaret was a top student, and one whose decorous behavior made her an excellent choice to act as a monitor for younger coeds. As a junior and senior, she was associate editor of *The Fisk Herald* (the student newspaper) and also served as head of the Young Ladies Lyceum, one of the school's three literary societies.

Her Tuskegee career began equally auspiciously, and when Booker T. was not away, he found himself more and more impressed with the attractive young woman and the way she became involved in the school's work, relieving him, as he put it, "of many burdens and perplexities." He was also aware of her in other ways—not surprisingly, since one newspaper report described her as having "beautiful features, arched brows, blue eyes, a Grecian nose," and went on to praise the carriage of her head, comparing it to that of the female exemplar of the day, the Gibson girl (then newly created by the pen of illustrator Charles Dana Gibson). Margaret was aware of Booker T. as well, and the increasingly personal tone of her letters to him—initially a means of keeping him abreast of campus news during his long absences from Tuskegee—reflects this. Exactly when the question of marriage was first raised between them is not clear, but there is no doubt that her changing relationship with him contributed not a little to some "burdens and perplexities" of her own.

One of the problems facing her was that Booker T.—probably

by nature and certainly by conditioning—was a formal man, somewhat aloof and unused to expressing his feelings verbally. Margaret apparently expected and wanted the kind of courtship he was unable to give her, one of warmth and spontaneity, complete with love letters of the type she knew he would be highly unlikely to write. She was troubled enough by the last point to try a little gentle extortion on him, saying at one time that she would not continue their correspondence unless he wrote her what she could consider a satisfactory letter. If there was a personality clash here, however, it was compounded by another, much more fundamental one in the person of Booker T's oldest child.

Margaret's efforts in behalf of Tuskegee, in which Booker T. called her "completely one with me," had of course brought her into contact with Portia, and with Baker and Dave. She quickly found herself disagreeing with the way in which the children were being brought up. Whether this was because of her developing feelings for their father or for other reasons of her own, it is interesting to note that the strongest disapproval she expressed in this regard was of Mary C. Moore, a white woman from Framingham, Massachusetts, who had been employed to care for the children temporarily. Mrs. Moore had been a friend of Olivia's.

There were others at Tuskegee with whom the forceful Margaret could not get along, and near the head of the list was Booker's brother John, who had been made Superintendent of Industries at the school. She found his manner generally objectionable, and wrote of him using such specifics as "false" and "spiteful." She was frank enough about expressing her thoughts and feelings, and she was candid about Portia. "You have no idea," she wrote to Booker T., "how I feel because I cannot feel toward her as I should. And I somehow dread being thrown together with her for a life-time."

"Dread" is a strong term to use about a child of ten, and in similar circumstances, another woman might have taken pains to hide her true feelings from her future husband, going to great lengths to present the situation in a more promising light. However, Margaret soon gave up whatever attempts she had been making to befriend Portia, deciding that "I will not let anyone talk to me of the child...and lose patience with her..." But she soon realized that could not conceal her feelings from the sensitive little girl, who was already well aware of the coolness between them: "She kinder [sic] understand it too and I hate it." Margaret did, however, continue to report to Booker T. on Portia's health: "Portia tells me that her nose bleeds every night and her stomach is often sick."

As the correspondence continued, she placed the responsibility of making the final decision squarely in Booker T's lap, telling him, "I shall be absolutely honest with you and if you feel that you prefer giving me up, I should find no fault with you. Don't be angry or annoyed."

It is possible that Margaret was using this strangely inverted honesty as a way of tightening the bond with Booker T. In any case, she finally ended the struggle with herself and agreed to become his wife. They were married in October, 1893, at Tuskegee, though she had hoped the wedding could be held in Chattanooga, Tennessee, where she had many friends.

Thomas Greene Bethune (Blind Tom).

SIX

"He expected a lot from his child"

When she decided to marry Booker T., Margaret had obviously also decided to make the best of a bad bargain where his children were concerned. But if she managed reasonably well with the boys, dealing with Portia proved to be a far less rewarding business. Indeed, what had begun as a kind of stalemate deteriorated rapidly and took on all the characteristics of a battle— varied only by the level of hostilities.

Portia's father was rarely at home, and even when he was, he did not take an active hand in his children's upbringing beyond occasionally allowing all three of them to sleep with him. The things that stay with children into later life often do so just because they were unusual. Portia's memory of how angry he once became because she could not "get" her arithmetic, and of how he came to her room later " to say he was sorry" has all the earmarks of one of these singular occurrences. Booker T. also did not speak to Portia about her mother—he may not have known that this was precisely what she badly needed at that time, or he may have thought that his silence on the subject would give the relationship between his new wife and his daughter a chance to improve.

His incessant absences in themselves provided sufficient reasons why he might had hoped that this was true. Many of the letters he received from Portia during this period are—on the surface at least—happy ones, concealing the turbulent conflict of

26

her emotions. After the Fourth of July, 1893—before he married Margaret—she wrote him the following account of how she spent the holiday:

Tuskegee, Ala. July 9th, 1893

Dear papa. You don't know how glad I was to secure your letter and was glad to have you tell me about Boston on the 4th of July. but we had a delightful time we got up in the morning happy as birds and I did my work then we went to breakfast after breakfast I washed dishes than I came up stairs and sewed then I went down stairs by that time it was dinner time and after dinner I washed dinner dishes then I came up stairs and played with Baker's ball until mama said I could go over to see Emma I sent over there and I helped Emma wash her dishes. I played with Emma and Gracie and Theodore and Horace. we shot some fire crackers. then I sent home and did work then it was supper time after supper I washed dishes. we had all ready fixed up our porch with drapery and flags....

The letter goes on to describe the rest of the day—the concert" held on the porch and how "Baker spoke a piece"—and ends by responding to her father's request that she tell him about the meaning of the holiday. It also includes the sentence, "I wish you could have been here."

The almost carefree (and careful) happiness of such a letter, with its use of the word "mama" and the charm of its childish misspellings, must have gone a long way to paint a falsely rosy picture for Booker T. He can hardly be blamed for believing that things were going well.

But they were not, and the situation was an unhappy one, worsening on both sides. Portia was rapidly turning into what Margaret called a "rather peculiar" child, often silent and withdrawn. She found this, too, difficult to understand, all the more so because her relationships with Tuskegee's girl students were—and always had been—excellent.

Against this background, anything that might have been part of the frictions of a normal growing-up process was hugely magnified, and the smallest issue could spark off a major outburst, which neither Portia nor Margaret was able to see in its proper proportions. One such explosion took place about a month after Booker T. and Margaret were married. Her new stepmother gave Portia what she still remembers as the worst scolding she ever received, because she had not cleaned her room.

There were more, similar incidents, and their increasing frequency only added to Portia's feelings of loneliness and insecurity, especially since other people did talk to her about Fannie. (One of them was Cora Varner, the widow of the man from whom the land for Tuskegee was purchased, in 1881.) Her real mother was dead, and it was easy—and comforting—to imagine that *she* would not have been like this. Now there were times when, no matter how hard Portia tried, the conflict with Margaret was too much for her to come to terms with. She could not cope with it alone and there was no one else to turn to, so she wrote to her father.

Sometimes I feel as if I have no friend in the world and I just cry, and Mama will say 'Portia what are you crying about' and I never tell her. I always tell you my thoughts because I think you would like to hear them.

There is room for speculation as to whether Booker T., both occupied and preoccupied with Tuskegee, liked hearing such thoughts from his daughter, but some of her efforts to reach out to him finally did have an effect. By the time she was twelve, Portia had almost decided to stop trying to please Margaret, except for those times when "...a book I read gave me better thoughts," and Booker T. had come to realize that matters could not continue as they were.

Things were complicated further by the fact that Margaret's approach to Portia's small half-brothers was quite different from the one she used with the young girl. It seems that the boys brought out other facets of her personality—those that have led even Portia to remember her as being "full of love" and having a "sense of humor." This was particularly true with the younger boy, Dave, whom she babied and seemed to favor. However, Portia still describes her home life at this time as "not a specially lively one," where there "wasn't much time for fun."

Nevertheless, Booker T. has also left his description of that home life, which he apparently enjoyed very much—albeit rarely:

"....the time when I get the most solid rest and recreations is when I can be at Tuskegee, and, after our evening meal is over, can sit down, as is my custom, with my wife and Portia and Booker and Davidson, my three children, and read a story, or each take turns in telling a story."

Other attempts at family togetherness were still being made—including Sunday afternoon treks into the woods to enjoy "the chirp of the crickets and the songs of the birds"—but these, too, were infrequent and more often had to do with Tuskegee. Perhaps outstanding among these was the trip to the Atlanta Cotton States and International Exhibition of 1895. All five Washingtons traveled to Georgia for this event, starting out from Tuskegee on September 17, the morning before.

Booker T. had already spoken in Atlanta two years earlier, and the favorable impression he had created on that occasion led to his being invited to address a mixed audience at the opening of the exhibition, which had attracted so much advance notice from both the press and the public, and of whose "responsibility" he was so conscious, that it gave him some of what he called the feelings of a man "on his way to the gallows." In his concern, he had gone over it with his wife and read it as well to the entire Tuskegee faculty.

Portia remembers another speech (at Tuskegee), "when my father had a lecture on." "It was raining heavily," she says. "He walked over to the place where he was going to lecture and carried an umbrella. He was so engrossed in what he was going to say that he walked down the aisle with the open umbrella over his head. One of the students took it from him."

Engrossed as he was in his Atlanta address, no such untoward occurrences marred it for Booker T.* Indeed, the speech brought

---

*It was during this speech that Booker T. told the story that is so often cited as the summation of his ideas. "A ship lost at sea for many days suddenly sighted a friendly vessel. From the mast of the unfortunate vessel was seen a signal, 'Water, water; we die of thirst!' The answer from the friendly vessel at once came back, 'Cast down your bucket where you are.' A second time the signal, 'Water, water, send us water!' ran up from the distressed vessel, and was answered, 'Cast down your bucket where you are.' The captain of the distressed vessel, at last heeding the injunction, cast down his bucket, and it came up full of fresh sparkling water from the mouth of the Amazon River. To those of my race who depend on bettering their condition in a foreign land or who underestimate the importance of cultivating friendly relations with the Southern white man, who is their next-door neighbour, I would say: 'Cast down your bucket where you are'—cast it down in making friends in every manly way of the people of all races by whom we were surrounded."

him nationwide attention and praise, and the prominence that followed in its wake was such that it extended to the White House. About a month later, President Grover Cleveland (to whom he had sent a copy) expressed his "delight" with the speech and included himself among those who "wish well for your race."

Portia's pride in her father now grew in its immensity, and it compensated—to a degree—for the lack of personal affection she was experiencing.

It was at this time that Tuskegee began to be a place Portia visited rather than where she lived. Her father knew that she was unhappy there, and partially because of Margaret and partially because he thought there were more opportunities for his child elsewhere, arrangements were made to send her away.

SEVEN

"She has unusual ability in instrumental music."

When Portia was twelve, she had already attended at least three schools—in various parts of the country and for varying amounts of time—in addition to the "children's house" at Tuskegee (a kind of laboratory or practice school for teachers-in-training). At the last she remembers being taught by "Lotta Young, who later married one of the teachers at Tuskegee, a man named C.W. Green." After her father's remarriage that year, Portia was enrolled in the Framingham Center for Grammar School Education—in the Massachusetts town where her first stepmother had received some of her education.

During her four years there, she was placed in the care of the same Mary C. Moore who had previously elicited Margaret's jealousy. The young Canadian woman taught English at the School and had family nearby—a sister named Mrs. Shaddock, who lived in the small manufacturing town of Hopedale. Portia spent some of her vacation time there.

For most girls, the early teens are sensitive, trying years, taken up with an anxious search for what will be their own way of life. Portia was no different, and she soon came to regard Miss Moore as someone who was "almost like a mother" to her—and as someone on whom she could pattern herself:

"You know, Bishop Lawrence of Boston [William Lawrence, Episcopal Bishop of Boston beginning in 1893] confirmed me at

31

Saint John's Episcopal Church in 1894. Miss Mary C. Moore, who had charge of me, was an ardent Episcopalian. She would take me to church every Sunday and it was through her that I joined.... My father remarked when I left the Baptist Church...that one could mark it down that anybody from the south who was not a Baptist or a Methodist had had someone tampering with their religion."

But Portia's love and admiration for her father were in no way diminished because of Miss Moore's influence, though they did for a time become somewhat confused with her religious feelings!

"I was also interested in the Catholic Church and at one time I thought of becoming a nun. For a while it was in my mind. I thought of how lovely it would be to be like a nun and Booker T. Washington's only daughter!"

In spite of Portia's statement that "I had almost no contact with Tuskegee during those days," all ties with her father—as its representative and embodiment—had not been severed:

"You know, my father spoiled me. He always wanted me close to him. He said that he received comfort out of me. I guess I rested him."

And, toward the end of her Framingham years, there were occasions when, if the path of one of Booker T's northern fundraising swings happened to cross his daughter's, she was included in his activities. Being with her father and meeting the "important people" he did might be helpful to her in later years—and because of her charm, since she was now a young lady, her presence might help him as well:

One of the greatest influences that my father valued was the contacts he made for me by introducing me to so many key people. Sometimes (they) would say...that I was a very precocious child.

So it was during one Christmas vacation a few years later, while Portia was in New York staying with school friends, that she "spent the morning visiting with Mr. and Mrs. Ignace Jan Paderewski....Mr. Paderewski was very fond of my father."

Whatever early press agent had been responsible for arranging the meeting, he must have been pleased with his efforts, and Paderewski may indeed have enjoyed Booker T's company. There were certainly some similarities between the two men, most obviously in the way both had achieved eminence after struggling long and hard to overcome their origins—origins that might permanently have shackled lesser men.

32

And the meeting with the Polish pianist-statesman, who was then at the zenith of his dual career, was significant for Portia, too. It meant a great deal to her, especially since she had discovered in music her own source of solace, one from which she had been "receiving comfort" for some time.

Exactly when the black piano virtuoso known as Blind Tom made his appearance at Tuskegee is not known. The young Portia was in the audience, however, and she recalls that "he played Liszt's Second Piano Rhapsody." She also remembers that "he didn't seem to know [how to read] music, but he could play anything."

Some of Blind Tom's antics puzzled her, however, and she was disturbed for a while by the apparent Svengali-Trilby relationship between his manager and him:

"This white man had him...was with him. He sat on the stage and was a sort of counselor. He seemed to have a hypnotic effect on Blind Tom. I don't know what it was. But I can remember as a child I used to wonder why that white man would always go around with him. But he was getting the money. He became very rich off Blind Tom."

Though she says that Blind Tom was "kind of off, you know," there is no question that the impact of his playing on her was tremendous and unforgettable. "I was so fascinated," she says today. "I had never heard any music like that."

It was to be an enduring fascination, and after the benchmark experience of hearing Blind Tom (who was described in one contemporary account as having small, plump hands with short fingers, and who owned a dog named Paderewski), Portia had some music lessons at Tuskegee, from a man named C.A. White: "He was from Australia and I took private lesson from him." The Fourth of July letter to her absent father 1898 gives some indication of how seriously she already took them, for she includes in that helter-skelter listing of the day's activities the facts that she "Practised" and "played the piano." Getting children to practice (whether the piano or another musical instrumentj) has been the bête-noire of many a patient parent. To the ten-year-old Portia, it was a matter of course, a feature of life as essential as washing dishes, and one which could not be done without.

Her musical training went on at Framingham, where she took lessons from "a Miss Hart, who lived in the village," and her talent (she believed it came from her mother's side of the family, which included a distant relative who sang professionally under the name of Madame Selicka) continued to develop. She began to acquire a considerable repertoire that took in many of the classics by such composers as Mozart, Dvorak, Chopin, and Bach.

But Portia's own insecurities still remained with her and caused her occasional problems. It must have been these—coupled with the natural shyness that any young person might feel when first asked to play in public as opposed to the family—that led her to refuse an invitation of Booker T's. She was about sixteen at the time, and her father had taken her with him to a reception given in his honor in Charleston, West Virginia. The former governor of the state may have been there, and other dignitaries certainly were. It was all too much for Portia, and she took refuge in the excuse that she was "not good enough."

In 1889, her four years at Framingham were over. Now she put in a year at Tuskegee, for some of the practical education whose value her father had always emphasized. (In his Atlanta speech, he had stated that "No race can prosper till it learns that there is as much dignity in tilling a field as in writing a poem.") She graduated with the class of 1900, having completed—among other studies—a course in dressmaking., of which she says today, "I hated it...I only did it for him."

Portia was seventeen in the spring of 1900. For many daughtters of good family" at that time, though musical ability was something to be encouraged—a ladylike activity on a par with embroidery, watercolor painting, and sewing—it was not something to be carried too far. There was travel, too, for such well-brought-up gentlewomen, and Portia remembers that "one summer my father gave me a trip to Nova Scotia." She was chaperoned on the Canadian excursion by Jane E. Clark, a "beautiful" and "spiritual" woman who was later to become Tuskegee's Dean of Women and a good friend of Portia's.

In a sense, all of these experiences were preparing her for an important step into a wider world. She was being readied for what could accurately be called her debut—as an individual in her own right.

EIGHT

"A Real Wellesley Girl"

Portia's debut took place in due course, but only after some more preparation—a second year at Tuskegee, this one as a music teacher. As Booker T's daughter she joined a faculty that then numbered about eighty, and became for the first time personally involved in her father's work. She sometimes took her meals with the other staff members in the large dining room in Armstrong Slater Memorial Hall. (If she ate there on her eighteenth birthday, she had a copious menu to choose from, for on that day breakfast alone consisted of oranges, oatmeal, fried steak and gravy, biscuits, and boiled grits!)

This period also saw the building of the colonial-style mansion called the Oaks—with its well-appointed interiors and such modern conveniences as three bathrooms and steam heat, a suitably imposing residence for the head of Tuskegee and his family. It was during this time, too, that Portia's relationship with her father moved onto an adult-to-adult level and she became someone he could talk to. He would use her as a sounding board, testing his speeches on her and "stopping" to ask, 'How does that sound?' And her relationship with Margaret had altered as well, subtly if not substantially. At least a part of the earlier difficulties had arisen out of Margaret's basic dislike of small children. Now a little surface equanimity had been achieved— at least enough for Margaret to "go to bat" for Portia in the matter of her wages at Tuskegee. "Principal's daughter" or not, once-dreaded

35

stepdaughter or not, a spirit of fair play had begun to prevail, and seven dollars a month was too little.

As the summer of 1901 drew to a close, the question of Portia's continuing education was discussed, and though there was some indecision as to which college she would attend, her ties with New England had by this time grown so strong that it was taken for granted that the rest of her schooling would be in that part of the country. Portia remembers that there were some problems about her college applications. It is possible that she was considered inadequately prepared or in fact, as she says, that she was simply "too late getting in Bradford." Whatever the reason, at some point she said "let me go to Wellesley." She may well have heard of the school while she was at Framingham—perhaps from Miss Moore or later, from Miss Clark though today she claims "I had no idea I was going to that great big college." But, she adds, "My daddy had so much influence (that) they accepted me."

The note of near-wonderment and awe that runs through her words must have been a good deal stronger that autumn. Portia still has an article from the now-defunct *Philadelphia North-American* describing her arrival and first weeks at college. It appeared on Sunday, November 3, 1901, and bore a headline reading "Portia Washington, Daughter of the Illustrious Founder of Tuskegee, Becomes a Real Wellesley Girl."

The piece begins, appropriately enough, with a report on Portia as Booker T's child, the daughter of a man who "in the step of one generation (had) made himself the leader of his race...." "When Booker T. Washington went to college," the rather breathless article continues, obviously quite sincere—if remarkably unsuccessful—in its effort to sound patronizing, "he tramped as a ragged, forlorn little black boy from a Southern Negro cabin to Hampton, where he helped pay his way through the institution by sweeping the floors and working...on holidays and vacations.

"When his daughter commenced her collegiate education the other day, he himself took her in a Pullman car to Boston and thence to the fashionable woman's college, where she was placed under the care of the dean with all the ceremony and distinction that is shown a millionaire's daughter.

"And she has been as carefully reared, this Negro girl, as any of Boston's own cultured children. It is evident in an air of good breeding...and a refinement of manner, which are as well marked as though her color were white.

"She is 18 years old, she says, but with her slim, straight frame and her skirt yet ankle length, she looks not more than 16. She is only a little school girl in her ways, scarcely yet a college young woman, very childlike and unsophisticated. One looks in vain for the qualities of independence and leadership which she might have been expected to have inherited from her mother, whose executive ability called her to the presidency of a national federation, and from a father who is the founder of Tuskegee. But there is no evidence, so far at least, that the little Wellesley girl has inherited any endowment from all of this achievement."

After praising Portia for her modesty, calling her as "quiet and unassuming" as the daughter of "an obscure drifter or railroad porter" (points of comparison of a disarming naivetè), the report continues with an interviewer's questions to Portia herself, regarding the "reputed 'color line' at Wellesley":

"You want to write me up, you say?' she replied in a mystified sort of way to a reporter recently.

" 'Why, what for?' she added, while the dazed expression on her face deepened.

"It was explained that the public might be interested in knowing something of her and hearing about her as about her father and mother.

" 'I don't understand,' she repeated. 'With Mamma, of course, it's different. She's a grown woman. But me, why, I'm only a little girl,' and she laughed at the suggestion that she could possibly be of any importance."

Important or not, "Miss Portia" was attractive in appearance, and the article goes on to say that "she is a very good looking young colored girl. She is almost beautiful; some people would call her quite so in spite of the fact that her features aren't as regular as they should be....They are not the Characteristic Negro features, however." Details follow:

"The full lips and the wide nostrils are conspicuous by their absence, and her complexion is several shades removed from black. She is quite a mulatto, in fact.

"But if the beauty of her face might be questioned there could be no two opinions about her hair. The glory of the night is in it, and

37

it is a crowning possession which any white girl might be proud of. It is raven black, of course, and as fine and shining as silk."

According to the *North-American*, that hair was worn simply, "fastened in a loose knot," and Portia faced the reporters with her eyes looking "shyly from beneath long, drooping lashes." Her voice was found so pleasing that it was called "one of her chief charms" and something which confirms the impression of refinement already conveyed in her bearing. It is soft and low and sweet, with all of that delicious Southern accent so musical to Northern ears....

"For college she dresses very plainly, in a gray skirt and jacket and a wash shirtwaist. All of them said she had devoted herself to an industrial course at Tuskegee. Besides being a practical dressmaker, she can trim a hat or bake a loaf of bread equally well, for she has also taken the courses in millinery and in housekeeping. All this is in accord with her father's belief that every colored boy or girl should have manual along with mental training."

The article continues with a description of the spare artistic environment in which Portia studied music:

"....her speciality, and all of the Negro love of music tingles in her finger tips. She spends two hours a day in practice on one of the pianos in the Music Hall. It is in a room on the third floor, like all of the others a bare little room with not another piece of furniture in it than the piano and stool and a tiny radiator....and by waxing lyrical about Wellesley's natural setting, in terms that might have been lifted bodily from one of the college's early catalogs, speaking of how the oaks whispered a "murmuring chorus to the blushing red-hued maples," and of how the playful chipmunks and squirrels who lived among the trees sometimes ventured forth "across the very path of the college girls, with whom they seem to be on most familiar terms."

At last the account returns to Portia herself, who seemed to find the vista equally entrancing—" 'I could stand for hours and look from this window'—if a little chilly: 'I suppose I will have to begin wearing a hat soon. I don't like the feeling of one, and at home I am without a hat but the air is so frosty this morning that I begin to think I can't do without it much longer' "

Just a normal college girl, and though neither she nor anyone else had taken the trouble to set the press straight on the subject of

Margaret's real relationship to her, someone had made her status at Wellesley plain enough. She was not a real Wellesley girl at all, but a "special," and the article gave that as the "real reason why she has rooms in the village instead of within the college grounds." She roomed with a Mrs. Brehaut in the town, and ate sometimes at the home of Professor Coman, who taught astronomy, and sometimes at that of Katherine Lee Bates, the professor of English who later wrote the poem "America the Beautiful."

Notwithstanding her separateness, Portia stated that the other students were "just as nice to me as they can be," a claim allegedly corroborated by the reporter, who gushed "...you can see them any day. They call on her and chum with her and invite her to their receptions and social functions. Last week she was made a member of the Young Women's Christian Association at the College."

So Portia was not aware of a "color line" at the college, and besides, there was only one other black girl enrolled there at the time, "Miss Charlotte Atwood, a junior, who lives at Stone Hall, and sleeps in the same building and eats at the same table with the other girls." (Even Portia was a bit breathless in this discussion of racial matters.) The article, however, found it a natural reaction (despite the earlier gushing corroboration of the generous spirit of the Wellesley girls) on the part of the Southern Wellesley girls that they did not seek out Portia and Miss Atwood in order to make friends with them, and that they adopted instead what it classed a "position...of neutrality."

This article, the result of what was probably Portia's first encounter with the press, gives a picture of what today seems an almost incredible innocence—rather like that of a fledgling bird newly (and precariously) flown from the nest but still blissfully ignorant of the many dangers that lie in wait outside. In its banalities and cliches, it also reveals—no doubt unwittingly—a great deal of the racial outlook and attitudes prevalent in the United States at the time, even in the so-called "liberal" Northern press.

The newspaperman had presented one fact clearly, however; namely Portia wanted to become a music teacher. In pursuit of that goal, she studied harmony and theory "with a Professor McDougall" and started German, as well as taking a Bible study course—very important for a girl from a home where, she says, morning and evening prayers were "never missed."

There was to be another problem with the newspapers (these based in Boston) when she left Wellesley, and she still maintins with considerable vehemence that their reports, ascribing her departure from the college to prejudice, were "not the truth...."

But whatever the reason, leave she did in the spring of 1902. And perhaps it was under some kind of cloud, for nine years later the following statement appeared in the *New York Evening Sun:* "Miss Portia Washington was a student in Wellesley in 1902 but she did not finish her course there. The reason given was that she failed to pass her examinations and that her leaving, so far as the faculty was concerned, was entirely voluntary."

She had been lonely and wanted out.

Portia's expense account written out by her father, Booker T., which was later found in his suit pocket.

40

NINE

"Stars fell on Alabama"

Among Portia's fondest memories of her father are those of how "affectionate and sympathetic" he always was with her, qualities that lead her to call him "the most thoughtful person I ever knew in my life." She remembers that Booker T. took considerable time from his busy schedule for her. He saw to it that he had a special physical education course in Boston, which it had been recommened she take; and he fretted as an anxious father might when she became ill in that city during a visit to him, and made sure of having the best medical advice possible.

And when they were not together, Booker T. would "constantly" send Portia books, a wide-ranging selection including such classics and old favorites as Aesop's fables, Greek and Roman mythology, Grimm's fairy tales, and tales of King Arthur and his knights. "During the summers," Portia says, "I studied German privately under Professor Talley from Fisk University. He and his wife would be at Tuskegee, and my father arranged for me to study the language under him....It was good training." The picture that begins to emerge is that of a concerned father who was taking care that his only daughter should have all the advantages that money—and his position—could procure, and that her path through life would be infinitely smoother than his had been.

When she was nineteen, that path led her to Bradford Academy, or as it became known that same year, Bradford Junior

College. Located in Haverhill, Massachusetts, in the extreme northeastern part of the state near its border with New Hampshire, the school ws even then one of the city's chief claims to fame (another was as a leader of the shoe industry). It was one of the oldest women's educational institutions in the United States and it enjoyed a reputation as prestigious as Wellesley's. Booker T's role as an educator and head of Tuskegee was helpful to Portia in this situation, too, for his fundraising work had made possible his meeting with Alice Freeman Palmer. Mrs. Palmer was the wife of a Bradford trustee, and it was she who paved the way for Portia's acceptance at the school.

Portia's memories of her three years at Bradford are pleasant ones, and she still enjoys a glance at the 1905 yearbook. Indeed, to riffle through its slightly yellowed pages is to take a trip backward through history to a time when college girls wore white, high-collared shirt-waists, long skirts, and upswept hairdos, and when their education was a far more leisurely and graceful procedure than it is today.

The Bradford Annals lists a faculty of sixteen, headed by Principal, Louise A. Knotts, who taught ethics and English literature. There were two other English teachers as well, and Portia remembers that hers was Jean A. Pond. She took Latin with Mabel I. Hart and continued her German under Fraulein Eva Salome Karrer. She also took art history, taught by the equally Teutonic-sounding Edmund von Mach (since he had a Ph.D., one wonders if she ever addressed him as "Herr Doktor").

And of course, Portia studied music. Bradford had two piano instructors during that period—Annie Louise Peabody and Samuel M. Downs, who had been at the school over thirty years and to whom the yearbook was dedicated. Portia says that Professor Downs was sufficiently impressed with her talents to arrange a partial scholarship for her, and her music lessons at college were free.

Many extra curricular activities were available to the girls, and they had opportunities to play basketball, tennis, or golf, or to join the Walking Club, whose Saturday tramps through the surrounding woods were a staple feature of Bradford life. There were also more serious student groups, such as the Christian Union, which met on Sundays and—probably through Portia's presence and efforts—set up a fund designed to help put a black student through Tuskegee. Guest lecturers were also invited to address the girls, including a fellow of the British Royal Astronomical Society and, in Portia's senior year, her father, who spoke on the subject of Negro education.

The *Boston Herald* and the *Boston Record*—as well as several other newspapers—described the Bradford graduation, which was held on June 14, 1905. The *Herald* referred to Portia as "the first colored woman to receive a diploma from the institution" and as "one of the most popular students at the academy in the four years of her stay," adding that "her father and step-mother were among the guests at the graduation exercises." The *Record* says that the commencement address was delivered by the Reverend Newell Hillis of Brooklyn, New York, and that the diplomas were conferred by the Reverend A.H. Little of Dorchester, Massachusetts. It continues with a mention of Portia's piano solo during the ceremonies, which won her "plaudits and encomiums from the audience."

Portia was twenty-two when she graduated from Bradford. Her college experience had broadened the base of her musical knowledge, added to her expertise in German, and given her as well a measure of much-needed self-confidence and assurance—at least among girls her own age. Now it was time for her to seek wider horizons.

The years during which she grew into young womanhood had brought many changes to her father also. Tuskegee was now more than an established fact; it was something the whole nation could— and did—point to with pride. It was a place where presidential visits (William McKinley's in 1898 and Theodore Roosevelt's four years later) were becoming commonplace, and a lodestar of international magnitude as well. (When Prince Henry of Prussia, the younger brother of German emperor Wilhelm II, visited the United States in 1902, the bearer of the pompous name Albert Wilhelm Heinrich of the House of Hohenzollern received a momento from Booker T.—an album of the plantation songs that both men loved.)

As for Booker T. himself, after the furor caused by President Roosevelt's White House dinner invitation (shortly after McKinley's assassination made him president in 1901) had died down to a degree, he continued to serve the president as an unofficial but trusted advisor on all racial questions. He became the head of a kind of "black cabinet," and there were other visits to the White House; on one of these occasions Portia accompanied her father and met the president's independent and outspoken daughter "Miss Alice," then striving to live a life of her own in the fishbowl atmosphere of the White House.

Booker T. was in more demand than ever as a lecturer, as was Margaret, who had become head of the Federation of Southern Coloured Women's Clubs and held positions of leadership in other national organizations. In spite of the fact that the Washingtons now had the use of two summer homes—one in South Weymouth, Massachusetts, and the other on Long Island—and in spite of the large contributions rolling in from such sources as Andrew Carnegie, their work for the school continued, and they were so busy that they could only get away rarely for a rest.

Early in 1899, unknown to either Washington, plans were afoot to remove both of them from this perpetual merry-go-round of Tuskegee—fundraising-Tuskegee. At one meeting in Boston, as Booker T. himself told it in *Up From Slavery,* he was found to be "unusually tired." Then someone asked him "In a casual way if [he] had ever been to Europe." Though the question "soon passed out of [his] mind," other moneys had been raised, with the provision that he and his wife "must go," for a European trip for the two of them. Once Booker T's initial reluctance was overcome—he was predictably unwilling to leave his work and also feared that the trip might leave the bad taste in other black mouths that he and Margaret were "stuck up" and "show off"—he found himself for "the first time in all those years...free from care" and full of a "feeling of relief." Thus, uncharacteristically unburdened, Booker T. and Margaret took perhaps their only holiday.

Portia had seen her parents off on the *Friesland* at noon May 10, 1899. Not six years later, she found herself a departing passenger in the Port of New York. For, within a month of her graduation, her immediate future had been settled—she, too, would go to Europe.

The idea of a "grand tour" was far from a new one, and the children of wealthy Americans had long been sent to Europe to acquire a little of the polish and sophistication the Continent was thought to offer. Such a trip might also serve another purpose in enlarging the scope of Portia's life. Miss Peabody of Bradford had

44

studied piano in Germany, training with the eminent Martin Krause in Berlin. Portia remembers that her former teacher "greatly influenced the decision that I should study under Krause," and that "she sent him a letter of introduction and that was how I got in with him." Portia's fluency in German was clearly another factor in that decision: "If I had studied French or Italian, it is possible that I would have studied in France or Italy instead of in Germany."

It may have been because it was the accepted thing to do; or because, as Portia says, "I had to have somebody. I didn't know anything about life; or simply because it gave Booker T. a way to keep a watchful eye on his daugher, but at any rate, she did not go to Europe alone. Once again her chaperone was Jane E. Clark. In addition to her duties as Tuskegee's dean of women, Miss Clark had been helping Booker T. with his other work and served as his ghostwriter in at least one instance (she wrote the preface to a volume of Negro melodies by Samuel Coleridge-Taylor). She also fitted into what was by then a well-formed pattern of Portia's—that of choosing mother-substitutes or female "ideals"—to the extent that Portia had been disappointed that Booker T. had not made her his wife instead of Margaret. (Miss Clark must have been quite indispensable to Booker T., for Portia remembers that he was "saddened" by her marriage to Leslie Pinckney Hill, who was then head of Tuskegee's English Department and later became principal of Virginia's Manassas School.)

The two women sailed on the *Germania* in the summer of 1905, and after their landfall, the trip began with "one beautiful month in England," where Portia "cultivated a love for strawberries" and stayed at the home of Samuel Coleridge-Taylor in the London suburb of Croydon. She remembers that the black composer, who had visited Tuskegee in 1903, was "just as simple and unassuming as he could be." The two women also traveled to the Netherlands, Switzerland, Italy and Austria before arriving in Berlin.

Martin Krause, who was to become her teacher, was then in his fifties and had already had a distinguished teaching career. A native of Saxony, he had come to the Stern Conservatory in Berlin in 1904, after studying with Liszt, founding the Liszt Society in Leipzig, and teaching in that city as well as in Dresden, Bremen, Munich, and for a time in Switzerland.

In spite of the letter from Miss Peabody, which had preceded her, and in spite of what everyone had assured her was her excellent

German, Portia went to her initial interview with Krause in "some fear and trepidation." But she soon found that she had nothing to fear—at least not in the language area. He spoke no English, but... my knowledge of German was sufficiently good that I had no difficulty in understanding him, and I think he understood me all right."

With characteristic German—Saxon—matter-of-factness, however, Krause came straight to the point of their meeting, and almost immediately asked Portia to play for him. She remembers that she "had come prepared for [an] audition," and that one of the pieces she had selected was Coleridge-Taylor's "Sometimes I Feel like a Motherless-Child." Her Krause can hardly have known or guessed the special meaning of this particular song for his prospective pupil when he took her on.

Thus, in 1905, Portia began to live the life of a music student in Berlin. But she was once again what might be called a "special." She was placed for the duration in the nominal care of Dr. Karl Axenfeld, "one of [Germany's] outstanding Christian leaders," a strong force in the Evangelical Christian movement in pre-World War I Europe, and the man who had translated *Up From Slavery* into German. She was also special by virtue of her blackness, which made her a considerable curiosity in Berlin. Her landlady at 58 Steglitzerstrasse, however, was kind and proved to be a friend, sharing with Portia some of her recipes for the specialities of German cuisine. (In fact, she had had Negro lodgers, or Pensionaire, before: in 1903, the future concert pianist Hazel Harrison—and her mother—had stayed there while she studied in Berlin.) Portia later took other rooms, at 30 Dessauerstrasse.

Berlin, when Portia lived and learned there, was a city perhaps as isolated behind walls of provincialism as it is now behind those of cinderblocks and bricks. As the capital of a German Empire created in 1870 by Chancellor Otto von Bismarck's policies of "iron and blood," it was a city fairly new to imperial and international power and one that was still "feeling its oats" as it adjusted to its new position. It was the bridge of a "ship of state" from which William II had dropped the pilot," preferring instead to steer his own course behind such figurehead prime ministers as Count Leo von Caprivi and princes Chlodwig Hohenlohe and Bernard Von Bulow.

Curiosity or not, Portia enjoyed being in the bustling German capital, though she had some trouble adjusting to the weather and came down with the flu—for which she followed an old local prescription, honey. She also did well in her music, though she had to "study more in Berlin than any other place." Krause made her "work on playing from sight reading," but she greatly enjoyed her lessons with him. Krause lived on Prinzregentenstrasse, in a solidly fashionable section of the city—a detail she remembers because of another (somewhat vague and romanticized) recollection that she was "accompanied to [her] pension one evening by the young crown prince, who frequently traveled incognito."* She also saw and heard some of the major luminairies of the musical world of her time, among them the sopranos Geraldine Farrar and Mme. Schumann-Heink, and pianists Josef Hoffman and Teresa Carreno (the South American performed Grieg's G-minor Concerto with the composer himself wielding the baton as conductor).

Her studies with Krause continued, and by the time 1905 drew to a close, the teacher-student relationship had developed into an excellent one. Under his intensive tutelage, (and that of his assistant, a Pennsylvanian named Henry Kloman Schmidt), Portia had become accustomed to her independence and turned into someone who was more and more willing to do things on her own—from something so small as riding the streetcars and shopping for clothes at Wertheim's, the largest department store on Leipzigerstrasse, to acting as a hostess: "I had the pleasure," she says, of giving a little dinner party for [Abbie Mitchell] at a hotel in Berlin." (The black singer and entertainer was then on a European tour and had become the "talk" of Berlin.)

She did, however, continue to write her father, as if to reassure him that she was still his child and that he still mattered to her. There were letters and postcards, too, like the one she dated January 16, 1906, which bore a picture of the church she attended in Berlin—the Amerikanische Kirche (American Church) on Motzstrasse.

In spite of the communication between them, however, there are indications that it must have seemed to those at home—especially, of course, to Booker T. himself—that Portia was growing further away from them than they had anticipated or liked. In the early part of that year, these "having a wonderful time, wish you

*In light of Prince William's penchant for liaisons that were extremely troublesome to—and from which he frequently had to be extracted by—his family, this is perhaps not so far-fetched a memory on Portia's part as it might at first seem.

were here" messages ceased to be enough. Perhaps they also feared that Portia was well on her way to joining the increasing number of expatriates—those Americans who found the European way of life so pleasing that they lived out their lives in one Continental city or another. At any rate, Margaret—accompanied by Dave—was dispatched to escort Portia back to the United States.

But there was more to the end of Portia's European sojourn than mere family considerations. Another person was involved, for she was also turning her sights homeward in order to take one of the most important steps in any woman's life—marriage.

TEN

"He was very much interested in me and wouldn't speak to me when he found out I was going to come home and get married."

Portia had first met William Sidney Pittman at Tuskegee some three years before. Eight years older than she was, the attractive young man had been born in Montgomery, Alabama, of a black mother and a white father. He showed such promise as an architect that he "was given money from Tuskegee as a loan" so that he could study at Philadelphia's Drexel Institute of Technology. A brilliant student, he "finished in three years [and] came back to Tuskegee and taught and paid every penny back...." Although Pittman (as Portia always called him) returned to Tuskegee as the bright star of what was known as the Mechanical Department, he had an abrasive personality, which caused him some problems with the head of the department.

He didn't like to have any domination over him. And there was this man who was supposed to be his superior...at Tuskegee. His name was Mr. Taylor. He graduated from M.I.T. [and] my father had a lot of confidence in [him].

Portia remembers that her father had developed a technique that she thought "so smart" for dealing with inevitable internecine conflicts that arose among his staff and students. When there was a clash between Pittman and Mr. Taylor, "my father would have them both in his office and say, 'Now you talk frankly to me, Mr. Pittman, and tell me just what you don't approve of. Don't come to me separately. Both of you straighten out your problems.' "

They met as many young couples did—through one of those combinations of accident and clever family plotting: "Around 1901 or 1902 my father had William Sidney Pittman design a mantel for our home. My father [knew] I might well become interested in Pittman." As the young architect worked on the design, he found himself increasingly attracted to the "young and fresh" daughter of the house, who was playing the piano.

I was playing the piece called "Narcissus." Pittman remarked how well he thought...I played. I smiled, and we had a drink of lemonade. That is how we met.

But although Portia's education was soon to separate them, it did not put an end to the budding courtship, and Pittman did not forget her. They met again whenever she visited Tuskegee, and at some time before she left for Europe he declared himself; she says it happened on the platform at Chechaw Station. So they had what was then known as an "understanding" and they were what in more recent times was described as "engaged to be engaged." He cannot have been out of Portia's mind for long either, for he soon began to press her for a definite decision, once writing her in Berlin that if things were not finally settled between them he would end their relationship himself.

If Pittman's persistence ultimately prevailed, it was not without a little help from Margaret, who seemed to like the young architect enough to plead his cause with her stepdaughter. Portia says today that her stepmother "loved him because he was light. She really almost made the match for me." And even when the decision had been made, the trip home was neither speedy nor non-stop. By coincidence or design—and how many young women before or since have similarly "used" time to reinforce a romance?—absence was allowed to make his heart grow fonder. Pittman had to wait another few months for his Portia, while she and her stepmother toured Europe. They made stops in Rome and Paris, but the westward journey was highlighted by a visit to Venice and Portia's second time in London.

In his novella *Death in Venice*, Thomas Mann described the same Venice that Portia saw. To him, as to so many travelers through the centuries, it was "this most improbable of cities," a place more imagined then real, where "dream towers and turrets rose from the waves" to offer the arriving visitor a "brilliant welcome." There was something about the air, in the rose-mauve of the city's protracted twilights and dawns, an atmosphere of a place where everyone has been before though they may never have left home.

Then as now, it was a city through whose winding, intersecting canals the visitor could be propelled in a gondola, journeying into another day (though its waters were then practically unsullied by the oil slicks of vaporetti, and it was not yet in imminent danger from mainland industrial pollution). It was a Venice where one could enjoy a leisurely tea (complete with delectable pastries) at Florian's—the stately cafe in the Piazza San Marco—watching the pigeons rise in a cloud of beating wings each time the Moors struck their gong or the sonorous tones of the towering Campanile rang out the changing hours.

Perhaps it was there, as the passing parade of Venice swirled around her, Margaret, and Dave, that Portia met Leo Ziffer. In spite of his German name, the young Italian (whose parents owned one of the city's countless glassworks) quickly became so enamored of Portia—and so importunate—that "he followed me all over Venice, even on to London. I had to tell my stepmother to [make] him stop following me....I knew I didn't intend to marry him because I could not marry outside of my race. Margaret or no, "Leo was so serious he threatened to have a vendetta if I did not marry him."

Portia was by then quite willing to let her stepmother "run interference" for her in romantic matters, and she says today that it had happened before, at home. "My love life was not interesting, because my stepmother was color-struck and always wanted me to have.... very light-skinned men." Back at Tuskegee, there had been Charles Winter Wood. As a little bootblack from Nashville, trying to earn his living in Chicago, he had become involved in the theater. By chance, his aptitude for memorization and declamation had attracted the attention of a wealthy manufacturer, who paid his way through Beloit College in Wisconsin.

Soon after he came to Tuskegee to teach elocution and drama, Wood met Booker T.'s child. "He dated me, but my stepmother didn't think he was the type of man that would make a good husband." Though Portia enjoyed Wood's attention, and adds that Margaret later "aided in getting my father to fire him," she herself had some second thoughts at the time. It is possible that the somewhat flamboyant Wood was not "masculine" enough for her, but she says today that she could not marry him because "my heart wasn't quite in it."

A diplomatic reception was held for Portia and Margaret at the Liberian Embassy in Paris. Among the guests in attendance were the

American and Haitian ambassadors to France and the artist Henry Ossawa Tanner, a resident of the city. (The black painter had studied and worked in the French capital for some years, making his reputation with religious subjects such as *Daniel in the Lion's Den*.) As a very small child, Portia had briefly attended a Philadelphia kindergarten, and stayed in the home of his father, Benjamin Tucker Tanner, who was a well-known Methodist bishop in that city.

And in England, they visited again with Coleridge-Taylor and his family, and Portia remembers that they lived in a "modest... home," where the composer did much of his work on "just a little upright piano....You would never know he was as great as he was."

When the two women at last returned home in the summer of 1907 to prepare for Portia's wedding, William Sidney Pittman again had to tap deep reservoirs of patience. The following announcement appeared in the September 19, 1907 edition of the *New York Age* (a black newspaper of the period): Mr. and Mrs. Booker T. Washington announce the engagement of their daughter, Portia Marshall, to Mr. W. Sidney Pittman, of Washington, D.C. The marriage is to be solemnized at Tuskegee Institute during the latter part of October." In fact, the marriage would not take place until the last day of the month.

From "The Tuskegee Student," published by "The Tuskegee Institute, Alabama, Saturday, November 2, 1907:

"THE PITTMAN-WASHINGTON WEDDING"

"The chief social event of the year at Tuskegee Institute was the marriage Thursday evening, October 31st, at 'The Oaks', Principal and Mrs. Washington's residence, of Miss Portia Marshall Washington and Mr. William Sidney Pittman of Washington, D.C. The whole affaire was simple and impressive in its dignity. The Electrical Division of the school transformed the entire ground of 'The Oaks' into a blaze of light of light by utilizing colored bulbs in the trees, among the rose bushes, hedges, and in the various nooks and corners. Similarly, on the inside of the house, decorations of grasses, ferns, wild Southern smilax, white roses, with multi-colored lights, made the interior most beautiful. A great canopy in the main reception room had been erected, and it was under this that the ceremony was performed by Chaplain J.W. Whittaker.

"Just before the wedding procession formed, Mrs. Washington and her son, Davidson, took their places to the right of the canopy. Miss Gertrude Washington played the solemn Mendelssohn Wedding March, and the ushers, Messrs. Nathan Hunt, John Washington, Jr., George Austin and G.W.A. Johnston led the procession. Then followed the groom elect and his best man, Mr. W.R. Griffin, of Washington, D.C., and, in the order, the bridesmaid, Miss Gertrude Watkins of Montgomery, Ala., and last the bride-elect, Miss Washington, leaning on the arms of her father, Dr. Booker T. Washington. After the ceremony, congratulations of the assembled guests were earnestly and sincerely bestowed.

"The refreshments were particularly dainty, chicken salad, rolls, cheese, and olives being served, followed by ice cream in the form of red apples, lilies, white and green colored pears, busts of famous characters, a particularly formidable looking affair, was accompanied with a great deal of merriment as slices were distributed to all of the guests.

"Many presents were received by the bride and groom, coming from all parts of the country, from distinguished men and women who were friends of Principal Washington, as well as from many of their own friends. Those presented by members of our own community were also beautiful and in many instances very valuable.

Miss Washington is a graduate of the Tuskegee Institute, received the school's diploma and also a certificate from the Dressmaking Division. She also took a short course in the Millinery Division. Afterward, she studied and graduated from Bradford Academy, Massachusetts, one of the oldest school in the country for young women, being one of the only two young ladies of the graduating class to appear on the program. The next year she went to Europe for two years of study under Professor Krause, of Berlin.

"Miss Gertrude Watkins, the bridesmaid, was a relative of Mr. Pittman's and had been Miss Washington's life-long friend.

"Mr. Pittman, as is well known, is a graduate of the Tuskegee Institute, and of Drexel Institute; Philadelphia. He was Tuskegee's instructor in architectural drawing for a number of years, severing his relations voluntarily two years ago to establish an independent office in Washington. He had already won a high place as an architect.

"The couple, followed by the congratulations of many friends who came here from other parts of the country, as well as of the whole Tuskegee Institute community, departed for their future home, Fairmount Heights, Washington, D.C., Friday morning, November 1st."

. . .

As the plans for it began to stabilize, Booker T. was taking his role as father of the bride very seriously, and whereas Margaret was all for the match, there is some evidence to suggest that he was not completely overjoyed to find himself in the position of "not losing a daughter but gaining a son." Portia's father hired private detectives to follow Pittman and check him out, "in order to see if he had any habits that were bad or if there were any reason why I shouldn't marry him."

One is tempted to think that at this point *any* prospective son-in-law might have provoked a similar reaction from Booker T., but perhaps he really did harbor some questions as to Pittman's suitability—questions that might well have arisen out of his own experience with Pittman's contentiousness. (He had once wanted to send the young man away from Tuskegee when he had been the instigator of having the boys shave their heads; only Margaret's intervention prevented this.) About a year earlier, Portia says, her father had still had a "desire to see me marry Robert Russa Moton," and he implemented that desire by "actually [offering] to pay the fare for the Moton boy to visit me while I was in Europe, with the idea that I might be attracted to him." These plans, which certainly bespeak some qualms or reservations on Booker T's part, failed to materialize, and the Moton boy never made the trip.

Whatever Booker T. had hoped might come of it, and whether his doubts were resolved or not, the investigation proved inconclusive and wedding preparations proceeded on schedule.

ELEVEN

"Who giveth this woman....?"

Portia cannot remember ever having taken part in the pleasures of "trick or treat" as a child at Tuskegee, but when her father escorted her down the winding staircase of the Oaks on the evening of her wedding on October 31, 1907—Hallowe'en—in a sense all four of the principals were wearing masks. There was Margaret, the "Lady Principal" of Tuskegee, the happy stepmother who "beamed with joy" because "she had wanted the wedding," and the gracious pillar of the community basking in her husband's reflected glory. There was Booker T., a man who stood at once at the pinnacle of his race and his profession, a proud *Paterfamilias* whose children attended the best preparatory schools (Booker T., Jr., the Wellesley School for Boys, and the Drummer Academy in Massachsuetts, and the Phillips Exeter Academy in New Hampshire; and Dave the Oberlin Academy in Ohio) and who had attained such dizzying heights that his daugher and son-in-law had received a wedding gift from the President of the United States.

When the ceremony and the reception that followed it were covered in the *New York Age*, the glint of tears that some guests had spotted in Booker T's eyes as he gave his only daughter in marriage was not mentioned. The report concentrated instead on covering the wedding as a social event, and on the young couple. As for them, when they turned up the aisle after their "very lovely wedding" on what had been a clear, bright day, it must had seemed that all the sunshine of a happy future had just dawned.

Years later, many people can scarcely remember their first year of marriage, finding it difficult if not impossible to say when, how, or even if, it actually began or ended. Those days are duly marked by the calendar, of course but their separateness is lost. It has long since merged with the myriad of tiny details that go into building a life together. For Portia, like so many other young brides, there were such portentious decisions as where to put the furniture, with the Steinway grand that had been her father's wedding present to her occupying a place of honor. Though she did not need to learn how to cook (her Tuskegee years had taken care of that), she had at least to begin applying her homemaking skills on a day-to-day basis, and she recalls that, barely a month after her marriage, "was the first time I ever cooked a Thanksgiving dinner." (She probably used the impressive "$100 set of silver" from Theodore Roosevelt, and it is possible that the turkey for the feast was supplied by Booker T.; during his daughter's Washington years, he frequently sent her such gifts, and once there was a "possum," which he may have garnered on one of those hunting expeditions that were a well-loved relaxation at that time.)

For Pittman, as for most young husbands, his main role was as breadwinner and his principal concern that of making his name in his profession. He had opened an office on what was then Louisiana Avenue, where he was later listed as a "specialist in steel construction." His excellence as a draughtsman had previously led to his winning "a contest for the drawing of the Negro Building at the Jamestown Exposition," and now his design "for a colored YMCA on 12th Street" was selected in another competition. In spite of the commissions that came in, Pittman also found time to design and lovingly supervise the construction of the couple's first home. He called the two-story house, with its spacious porch "Little White Tops." Built in the Fairmount Heights section of Washington, on what was then called 61st Street and was later renamed Eastern Avenue, it was actually just across the Maryland state line—as Portia says, "so he could vote." (Residents of the District of Columbia did not receive the right to vote in federal elections until the 22nd Amendment to the Constitution was passed. Portia herself, of course, could not vote because of her sex—a situation that was only to be remedied by passage of the 19th Amendment after World War I.)

By far the most important event of Portia's first year of marriage was the birth of her first child—a child named, like his father, William Sidney Pittman—on August 17, 1908. But in spite of all the changes in her life, her interest in music remained a constant, and even as her pregnancy advanced, she continued her work in the field. Now she became involved in helping other members of her race to climb the musical ladder as she had.

Composer and arranger Harry Burleigh was one of her acquaintances at this time, and there was also a young music student named Clarence White, with whom she "got to be good friends" when he came to her home to practice. White, who later became "a great violinist," was just one of the many black musicians training with Madame [Azalea] Hackley—a well-known chorus director who was instrumental in giving them their start. In Washington, Madame Hackley and Portia worked together: "We gave his big concert at the Metropolitan Church and I was pregnant with my first child, but I managed to play three pieces on the program."

Portia again played "Sometimes I Feel Like a Motherless Child," and an "Etude by Sère," a French 19th century composer whose real name was Jean Poueigh, that she thinks is "out of print now." Her third selection may had been Chopin's Revolutionary Etude, but whatever her contribution, the concert was quite successful, and Madam Hackley "got enough to send [White] to Europe" to pursue his studies. Thus, as a young wife and mother-to-be, Portia was also moving in her own way into her father's sphere. For her, of course, the activities of helping other black people were not primary, but they were essential nonetheless.

Dr. Austin M. Curtis, whose offices were on 13th Street, had delivered Portia's first son on October 3, 1909, and he presided at the birth of the second, who was called Booker T. Pittman. And finally a girl, Fannie Virginia Pittman, was born to the couple on May 16, 1912. "Little White Tops" soon echoed with joyous sound of small children—sounds that often brought Booker T.—sometimes accompanied by Margaret—to Fairmount Heights. Portia points with pride to her photographs of Booker T. with his grandchildren in his lap—frozen moments from another era. It was a time when the precept "children should be seen but not heard" was widely accepted and put into practice, but apparently not with the little Pittmans. The photographs come to life as Portia comments that she can remember her father saying that if his grand-daughter went on as she had begun she sould soon have to be muzzled. (When the little girl sang for him, however, he predicted, "she's going to be wonderful") She also recalls her father giving William Sidney Pittman, Jr., a five-dollar bill, which the child promptly tossed into the fireplace, exclaiming "Pretty fire, pretty fire!" (One wonders with some amusement how Booker T. reacted to this evidence of his grandson's cavalier attitude toward money.)

It is more than likely that Pittman misunderstood the reason for Booker T's frequent visits, and that he may have believed their purpose was as much for his father-in-law to "keep tabs" on him as to take pleasure in his grandchildren. At any rate, he found them an irritant. (In this he was not unique, and such situations have been repeated throughout history, cutting across all cultural and social settings. In fact a few years before Portia studied in Wilhelmine Berlin, the tragically short life of Emperor Frederick III was also marked by such dissension. His wife, Queen Victoria's eldest daughter, idolized her father, and for a long time saw everything in terms of Prince Albert's responses.) No young man likes to hear—or can for long put up with—statements prefaced by "Poppa says," or "my father always..." before they begin to grate on him, building up a backlog of resentment. Against such a background, normal marital tensions are easily heightened.

So it was that in 1913, when an offer arrived from Dallas, Texas, for Pittman to design a temple for the black Knights of Pythias in that city, fate or circumstances seemed to be playing into his hands in providing an opportunity for change. Perhaps a thousand miles across the country—and away from Booker T.—he and Portia could achieve a better, more solid relationship.

TWELVE

"I thought we had left seriousness behind in Europe...."
Henry James, *The Europeans*

In 1913, the Pittmans "Pulled up stakes," renting out "Little White Tops" and shipping most of their furniture—including, of course, the Steinway—to Dallas. Portia says that they "first lived with friends....I wonder if the street is still there, by the name of Roseland Avenue." Later, they "had a small cottage on Juliette Street" and finally the family of five moved into an apartment at 1018 Germania Street, between Ross and Jacinto streets. (After the outbreak of World War I, in an atmosphere of loathing for all things German in which dachshunds were stoned and German measles were renamed, it would be called Liberty Street.) There Portia remembers that they "did very well at first," and Pittman designed, in addition to the Pythian building, "several churches all over the state," as well as "homes in San Antonio and Houston, too."

The young couple becamse involved in community activities, especially in the church. In January, 1914, Pastor S.E. Watson of Dallas' Macedonia Baptist Church wrote to Booker T.: "I have just had the pleasure of baptizing your daughter, Mrs. Portia W. Pittman into this church, and she has been elected as its Organist and Musical Director. Mr. Pittman is a Deacon and Trustee in the same church." Six months later, Reverend Watson was still pleased with their efforts, and wrote to Booker T. again: "Mr. and Mrs. Pittman are giving splendid service in church work here."

But Pittman's attitude toward his work created problems for them. "He was so exacting," Portia says, "and difficult to satisfy [that] the men who worked with him would get to dislike him...." Indeed, the architect had become so intense and hard-to-please that "he reached a point where he did not get any work."

Portia, too, was working—at a job teaching music in the Dallas public school system. Even today, when women's liberation has reshaped so many people's ideas, some couples have difficulties adjusting to a situation in which one's partner's professional "star" is on the ascendant while the other's is—if only temporarily—burning dimly. In those days, the whole women's movement was still, for all practical purposes, in its infancy. Pittmen's pride was wounded when his wife "had to bear most of the expenses from [her] jobs," and when to her willingness to share the financial responsibilities was added the need for her to do so.

But, because she had "the children to keep," Portia continued at her job, working "very, very hard" as a high-school choral director and taking on as well a "large church choir." It cannot have been an easy time for her, and she must have worried a great deal as she carried on her duties, refining young voices and listening to their sounds. The greatest source of her worries were her three small children. Though they would soon be old enough to start school, they were still living in a brooding, unhappy atmosphere.

As his architectural commissions petered out, Pittman had become an embittered man. Any slight—genuine or imagined— would prey on his mind, festering there and feeding the already large burden of anger he carried within him. Always volatile, he now became even more so, and was quick to flare up and lash out— verbally and sometimes physically. Portia realized—and feared— that her children might suffer from constant, prolonged exposure to their father's misery. Everything had altered drastically in the years since her marriage in 1907.

The world was changing, too, in many ways. Before the sinking of the *Lusitania* in 1917 finally brought the United States into World War I, automobiles had largely replaced horse-drawn carriages, many homes (including Portia's) were equipped with telephones, and the airplane had become an accepted weapon of war.

. . .

In 1915, Booker T. was 59 years old. Personal considerations had always taken second place to his work, and if his daughter now wrote to him, unburdening herself of her troubles, the downward course her marriage had taken would have been no exception. Mercilessly driving himself as hard—or harder— than he ever had, he was still bent on ensuring that, though he might die, Tuskegee would live on as his monument to posterity.

Indeed, his selflessness where the school was concerned was such that in 1900, when Andrew Carnegie offered him a gift of $350,000 as part of a larger donation to Tuskegee, he refused and changed the terms of the offer, accepting instead the whole $600,000 for the school, which he would bequeath to the nation. There would be no personal gift—no—thing to be handed down to his family that he had not attained himself.

He had now given himself with like singlemindedness to this cause for more than a quarter century. In all those years, any periods of relaxation had been enforced, fleeting, and ineffective, largely because he was a man who was fundamentally incapable of "dropping all now and then." Even his occasional hunting trips to Nearby Coden, Alabama, with such cronies and fellow-members of the "black cabinet" as Robert Terrell and James Cobb, were only functions of his role as a presidential adviser.

In the process, the strain had grown so great that Booker T. had been worn down past the point at which there might had been any possibility of reversal. Portia says that her father suffered from "poor circulation—arteriosclerosis"—but adds that it was "hard work that [just] burned him out." He was now so tired that some reports stated that a nurse had to accompany him on his fund-raising forays, seeing to his needs and enforcing the special diet he had been ordered to observe. But all these efforts proved to be futile, and in 1915, while he was in New York, Booker T. collapsed completely. When the doctors held out no hope of recovery, he voiced his wish that he might be allowed to die in the place to which all of his adult life had been devoted.

A special train was arranged to carry him home to Tuskegee for the last time. Watched over all the way by his faithful "masseur" and general factotum, a former Tuskegee student known as "Mr. Poaches," Booker T. arrived on the afternoon of November 13, 1915. He died early on the morning of the 14th, finally attaining the rest he had never found in life.

When her adored "poppa" passed away, Portia was there, for she had put her own cares aside in order to be at Tuskegee to await his return. The moment-by-moment dying of a parent—especially one so beloved—is often etched into the memory for life. The outlines of a bed, a room, and of other people's words and faces, may remain long after their actual details have faded, because they were eaten into the mental "plate" by the acid of pain. Portia remembers Booker T's death like this:

"I was there at the Oaks waiting for him to come by train. The train brought him all the way from New York; there had been arrangements made with the New York Central to have his car come all the way to Tuskegee without any change, and there was a car waiting...to drive him to the Oaks. My stepmother, Dr. Kenny (John A. Kenny, Booker T's doctor), Miss Jennie Armstrong, and I were all there in the room....He died in my arms...."

Such are the simple words—no more than a factual report—that Portia uses to describe the greatest loss of her life. But even in her grief, she did not lost her self-possession and, more important, her sense of what was the right thing to do in a given situation. Immediately after her father died, Portia says, she "ran out and notified the other officers of the Institute before the word got out into the papers."

As soon as the word did get out, however, messages of sympathy and condolence began flooding into Tuskegee. Some 8,000 mourners attended the funeral three days later, which was conducted principally by the school's chaplain, J. W. Whittaker (who had married Portia and Pittman just eight years earlier). As they heard the measured strains of Chopin's Prelude in C Minor, the bereaved family could take pride in the size of the congregation for the funeral, and in the tributes and words of praise that came from the national press—especially from the Southern papers. These spoke of Booker T. as an "exceptional genius," with a "brain and heart of the finest quality," who "worked with the forces about him" until he achieved a "prominent place...for himself in the world" and a "commanding situation" for Tuskegee. "No man" said the *Macon Telegraph*, "has done so much for his people...."

For Portia, her stepmother, and half-brothers, there was some comfort in the fact that Booker T. "wasn't in any pain" when he died. They could rejoice, too, in their personal memories of the man. They could recall those things in which he had taken pleasure, such as riding. This was a sport he pursued almost every day when he was at Tuskegee, on his horse, Dexter—who Portia is certain was not named for the well-known street in Montomery. She can still visualize what took place before those early-morning rides, when Mr. Poaches would "call over to the horse barn...for Dexter to be sent over." The horse was so well trained that once he had been saddled and bridled, says Portia, "he would come over to the mounting block at the Oaks by himself," There Dexter would stand, neighing and whinnying, until Booker T. emerged from the house to give him the lump of sugar he knew he could expect. Then, "if he wasn't ready to mount immediately, he would tell him to go off and graze until he was."

The bond between Booker T. and Dexter was apparently one of those rare ones, in which a special communication and understanding is established between man and animal. Portia's recollection of what happened the night her father died supports this. She says that Dexter was usually a "docile animal," but on the evening of November 13, before the special train bearing the dying Booker T. to Tuskegee had even arrived:

"Dester was instinctively disturbed. (He) broke loose and out of the barn, and with one neigh following another, he came to the mounting block at the Oaks. There was something weird and uncanny in his neighing that night, before my father died."

For the Washingtons, there were many more happy memories of Booker T. and the things he had loved. Hunting and fishing had been among these, and in fact he had never lost what was really a farm boy's almost instinctive feeling for the simple things of the earth. In *Up From Slavery*, he tells us that he kept pigs and poultry, and that raising them gave him a "great deal of pleasure." This was especially true of the pigs, and he goes on to say that "few things are more satisfactory to me than a high-grade Berkshire or Poland China Pig." The mental image of her father at "that kind of work" still brings a smile to Portia's face, and she deeply regrets the loss of a photograph of Booker T. as he "went around picking up eggs."

She can also remember that her father was sometimes what she calls "very jokey," and that he liked to use touches of humor to underline or drive home a point in a speech or discussion. She says, too, that he loved music—especially the old Baptist hymns that he first heard in his childhood, long before he changed the world for himself and other Southern blacks, but also pieces by Chopin, Dvorak, and Beethoven—anything with force and feeling."

Her other, more cherished memories are of the times when the relationship between herself and her father was a warm and tender one; the times when as a small child, she would climb into his lap with the demand, "Now read me a story" (one of her favorites was Washington Irving's *Rip Van Winkle*). And she is even happier that, before he died, Booker T. was able to repeat that experience with *her* children.

Thus, the father that Portia remembers was a vital, many-faceted human being. There was at least one instance, however, in which an aspect of his "humanity" led to results more troublesome than tender:

I have heard several people say that my father ran after white women. They have said that he was often assaulted (because of this). I know that my father was a very normal man and that he loved women, but I have never believed that or any of those stories.

Portia's version of the best-known of "these stories" follows:

My father was viciously assaulted by Harry Ulrich...in front of (Ulrich's) home (on West 63rd Street) in New York on March 19, 1911....Ulrich said that he had mistaken (my father) for a burglar and that (my father) had annoyed his wife. My father denied this, and explained...that he was looking for the residence of the auditor of... Tuskegee....Ulrich was arrested on my father's charge of assault.

...My father was brought into the West 68th Street police station by a policemen who had chased him up Central Park West after a scuffle in the hallway at Ulrich's house. After the two men had told their stories, the charge of unlawful entry against my father was dismissed, and Ulrich was held (for) assault. He gave $500 bail....

After my father was assaulted, he was taken to Flower Hospital. It seems...he did not stay there long, but recovered at his hotel....His scalp was cut in two places, his right ear (was) split, and his face was badly bruised....(but) he made two speeches three days after he was attacked.

Ulrich was continually getting his trial postponed. In October...
three of (his) witnesses could not be found, and the trial was postponed to November 6, 1911.

In the interim, the case—which finally resulted in Ulrich's
acquittal—was blown up into sensational proportions by the press
around the country. President Taft wrote to Booker T., and Portia
says that he expressed his regret at the notoriety" surrounding her
father's involvement in the case. But there were others who were not
at all sorry to see Booker T's image tarnished, and she says that Ulrich
received many contributions and letters of support from "Southerners who resented my father."

Repercussions were still being felt a year later, when Booker T.
publicly denounced the behavior of heavyweight prizefighter Jack
Johnson (the "Great White Hope"), saying that Johnson's actions
went against what "countless good and honorable Negroes had done
to build up their race." "For what it may be worth," Portia says (and
her tone leaves no doubt whatsoever of her opinion), "Johnson said of
my father, 'And as for Booker T. Washington, I never got caught in
the wrong flat. I never got beat up because I looked in the wrong
keyhole.' "

By November 14, 1915, however, the Ulrich incident had been
forgotten, and Booker T. was universally eulogized as a man whose
shoes would be practically impossible to fill. For his family, there
were only sorrowfully loving memory and pride in Tuskegee. And for
Portia, there were other claims on her emotions: William Sidney
Pittman, Jr., Booker T. Pittman, Fannie Virginia Pittman—and their
father.

THIRTEEN

"The grief that I hear is my life somewhere."

Portia returned to Dallas to shoulder once more what had become a crushing burden. When she says today, "I love beautiful things; I don't like hard drudgery; I don't like to get on the floor and scrub; I don't like to wash woodwork. I have never liked that kind of work in my life," it is the voice of hard experience that we hear, and the memory is alive. When she adds, "I like for people to do it for me," it is in full knowledge of the time when there was no one to "do it" for her, as there was no one to do anything else—especially raising her children.

By 1920, when the "Great War" had become a thing of the past, they were growing up. Her oldest son, his father's namesake, was developing into a soft-spoken, well-mannered boy who made good progress in school and brought home report cards with the kind of good and excellent marks that any parent would have been proud to sign. But 10-year-old Booker T. Pittman, on the other hand, gave his mother great cause for concern. He did not apply himself and she feared for his future because there seemed to be no way to make him take an interest in his schoolwork. Little Fannie

Virginia's health was also a problem—she had begun suffering from mild, epileptic-like seizures. (Portia suspects now that a blow the child received from Pittman may have triggered the illness.)

All of these worries were Portia's alone to bear. Pittman was really no more than a presence, and now, as he sank deeper and deeper into his private morass of depression, "he drank heavily" as well. But if Pittman tried to lose himself in alcohol, his wife instead threw herself into her work—trying to find there the pride, the response, and the sense of building something for the future that she knew were irretrievably gone from her marriage. She remembers some of the youngsters she taught in those days:

One of my pupils was Buddy Johnson, who (later) arranged all the music for Earl Hines. And Buddy tells on one of his records how I helped him. Buddy, Treseyant Sims, and all that bunch in Dallas. I taught them harmony and theory. They were a bright group....I divided them into sopranos, altos, basses. I had them learn songs...separately, in sections. One that was popular was the old Welsh song, "Men of Harlech."

As the years passed, her contributions to her field grew in magnitude and she achieved considerable recognition, though she maintains "...when I was in Dallas they did not like to have married women, but I could do some things that a lot of them could not do, so they made an exception in my case. Every year I would get a raise in salary, and then, when I had that 600-voice chorus down there, it made quite a sensation."

It did, indeed, and the occasion was a convention of the Department of Superintendence of the National Educational Association, held at Dallas's Park Auditorium. Portia led the chorus in a program including such spirituals as "Oh, Mary, Don't You Weep, Don't You Mourn," and glowing reviews were featured in the next day's papers. The accolades in the *Dallas Morning News* on March 2, 1927, were typical:

...A chorus of 600 Negro high school pupils sang a dozen old favorite selections with Portia Washington Pittman of Dallas, daughter of the late Booker T. Washington, as their conductor. It as a musical concert such as is seldom heard even by the Southerners and that the chorus took its audience by storm was unmistakably evidenced by the applause after each number. (It must have been an additional source of pride for Portia that the school where she worked had been renamed in her father's honor.)

But, Portia says, there was no applause from Pittman, who still "didn't like the fact that I was working." He liked even less the fact that that summer, his wife went north to New York City, to take a course in conducting at Columbia University. It meant that she was still able to make a life of her own, based on abilities and interests, that excluded him completely.

It was during Portia's stay in New York that a great professional opportunity came her way—a chance to extend herself still further and achieve a larger reputation in music. "While I was at Columbia," she explains, "I got a telegram to come and teach at Langston University (a small, state-owned college in north-central Oklahoma)." But Portia knew that accepting the Langston—or any other similar—offer was out of the question now, so she regretfully turned it down. When the six-weeks' course was over, she returned once more to Dallas.

In New York she had felt herself part of the bustling, renascent black musical world, and had met some of its major figures—composers such as John Wesley Work and J. Rosamond Johnson—and shared in many mutually inspiring exchanges of ideas. Back in the home that was no home, she was reluctant to give up the recharging stimulus that such contacts had given her, and tried to "cast down her bucket" where she was.

When the black composer Robert Nathaniel Dett (known principally for his use of spirituals in choral settings) arrived in Dallas from Virginia, his work and Portia's naturally drew them together:

He was teaching at Hampton (Dett was director of music there) and he came to Dallas to direct some kind of a music festival. I had a group called the *Aida Choral Club*. I had them sing his Music in the Mine—a beautiful thing—and he gave me some interesting pointers. We got to be very good friends.

Though their friendship was only a professional one, to the jealous Pittman it seemed to give additional force to the wedge already driven between himself and his wife. The conflict over Dett grew worse when Portia offered the composer and another young black the hospitality of her home for the duration of their stay in Dallas.

"...I have given them a big room in my house. We have a very big house." Portia continues with some of that understatement so characteristic of her, "but my husband was sort of cranky." He was also not the sort of man to allow anything to run its course or even to let matters rest where they were, so when "Dett would spend the day up there...with this young fellow, my husband would say, 'I'm going to put that nigger out of here.' " In spite of her husband's threats, however, Portia refused to eject Dett, and he and his companion left only after the music festival was over.

Pittman's reactions to the situation, and his use of the word "nigger" in reference to Dett offer one more clue to what was happening to him. Indeed, Portia believes that most of her husband's problems were racial in origin, and that the selfsame light skin that had once made him—in Margaret's eyes—such a desirable marriage prospect for Portia was the largest element in the mass of ugliness that was torturing him.

His career had moved from a brilliant start to blighted stagnation, and where once, she says, "he could get work from white or black," now there was nothing. Not only was the door of professional acceptance shut tightly in his face (and he himself had helped pull it to), but because of his fairness he felt doubly rejected—among his own people as well—and "...he got so he disliked Negroes."

At about this time, when what Portia describes as his eccentricity must already have crossed the line into paranoia, Pittman's wrath against the world found a new channel. "...Instead of him doing something else," she remembers, "He started a newspaper and called it *The Brotherhood Eye*." Whatever bits of gossip (something Portia despised as much as her father had) came his way, he seized upon, blew up, and printed in the new vehicle for his fury. The newspaper rapidly acquired a highly unpleasant aura—"it was a scandal sheet"—as Pittman used it to pour out his bile upon anyone and everyone. "He was so bitter," Portia says, that he could not be stopped, not even when "one Negro tried to kill him." Although his own anger often ricocheted to strike him, he continued undeterred. No one was immune from his attacks, and so indiscriminately did he choose the victims of his "journalism" that he "talked about everyone in (the paper), even the principal of the school where I worked."

To add to Portia's troubles, it was from that school (and that unhappy home) that Booker T. Pittman "ran away" in 1927. He and several schoolmates—including Buddy Johnson and Treseyant Sims—had earlier formed a band called the Blue Moon Chasers, which played at school dances, picnics, and similar functions in the Dallas area. His mother says today that she had no idea where her son "got his jazz gift," since she "never played it at home" and did not even like its predecessor, ragtime. But it *was* the Jazz Age, and Portia admits now that it was natural that her son "just picked it up." At any rate, chasing his own "blue moon," "he followed these orchestras up to Kansas City." There he played soprano and alto saxophone and clarinet in several bands, including one led by Count Basie, and made a name for himself with his "forceful, dynamic attack."

Her oldest child was also away, though his life seemed to be following a more sedate path. Admitted to Howard University in Washington, D.C., in 1927, William Sidney Pittman, Jr., was successfully acquiring the credits toward a B.A. degree.

Portia had now spent years trying to hold together the unraveling strands of her life with Pittman. She had done everything of which she was capable and more, but it had not been enough. "Pittman kept on writing his scandal sheet. He did not pay any attention to his wife, and indeed, his writing in *Brotherhood Eyes* was making her position as a teacher untenable. Thus, finally, with only 11-year old Fanny Virginia still at home, Portia was forced to make a long-postponed decision.

Left to Right-Mrs. Gloria Davidson Washington-Jackson, Edith Olivia Washington Johnson, Margaret E. Washington Clifford, and Agnes Louise Washington O'Neil.

FOURTEEN

"I did love Pittman so much"

Though it was inevitable that Portia should eventually leave Pittman, it was nevertheless the hardest thing she had ever had to do. When she speaks of their separation today, her calmness belies the agony it cost her nearly fifty years ago. In fact, the tears still lie perilously close to the surface, and in any prolonged discussion of her husband—despite such comments as "I have not forgotten about... Pittman...(but) I guess we must learn to live with a little pain. That is what the world is made of"—her tiny smile and forcedly casual expression are those of a child willing itself not to cry before a stranger.

And there is only sorrow in her voice as she related the rest of Pittman's life story—"later he was put in jail for his journalism...(and) was shipped to Leavenworth, Kansas"—and explains that it was through her efforts that his sentence for libel was commuted by Franklin D. Roosevelt:

I had met President Roosevelt in 1939....I saw him and got Pittman out of prison, but we did not live together. He went back to Dallas and lost his eyesight and took up with a black woman who took

72

care of him and he lived with her and died with her. I did not even go to his funeral.

When FDR visited Tuskegee on March 30, 1939, addressing students and faculty from his car, Portia was enabled to intercede with the President through her acquaintance with his black valet, "a man named McDuffie and his wife. They made it possible for me to meet President Roosevelt."

But in 1928, all this lay far in the future, and Portia's primary concern was with the immediate resolution of her own life. She knew only that for Fannie's sake—as well as her own—it was imperative that she leave Dallas to chart a new, independent course for herself elsewhere.

In a curiously ironic sort of coming full-circle, that course let her straight back to Tuskegee. Portia now says simply, "when my husband and I separated, Dr. Moton invited me to come to Tuskegee." It was an additional irony (of which she makes no mention) that the "Dr. Moton"— in 1915—was the same Robert Russa Moton whom Booker T. had once been ready to send to Europe as a "red herring" to distract her from Pittman. Now his offer of a teaching position provided her not only with physical distance but also with the opportunity to achieve some emotional distance from Pittman and his problems. "Moton said, 'We're trying to get (William Levi) Dawson to build up our music school at Tuskegee' but Dawson was so temperamental in making up his mind. So Moton said to me, '...see what you can do.' ....He told me to take charge of the choir."

The Tuskegee to which Portia returned in 1928 was a different place from the one she had known. Many of the old faces were gone, and of her family, only her younger half-brother Dave was at Tuskegee when she came back. (Margaret had died in 1926, after devoting the last years of her life to her work in the National Association of Coloured Women"; and Booker T. Washington, Jr., was a successful real-estate broker, raising his family in California.) In general, cooly business-like efficiency had replaced the warm personal atmosphere prevalent in Booker T's day.

Some of those who had known her father were still there, however. One was the eminent black scientist George Washington Carver, whom Booker T. had brought to Tuskegee in 1896. Carver's work in introducing soil-enriching crops such as peanuts and sweet potatoes to Southern cotton farmers, and his development of countless new uses for these crops had earned him a reputation almost as formidable as Booker T's. But Portia remembers Carver, who "sat by me at the table every day when I went back to Tuskegee to teach," as gentle, self-effacing, and so wrapped up in his work that to outsiders he would seem "a very insignificant man." He often spoke with Portia during meals, sharing with her some of his wealth of information about the plant world he knew so well. She remembers that she and Carver, whose nickname was "Fess" and who "always seemed to wear the leaf of a plant of something," sometimes talked about Booker T., whom Carver had loved and with whom he claimed he could still communicate.

Portia's recollections indicate that her workload as a faculty member was not made any lighter because of the fact that she was Booker T's child, and if she had hoped to be so busy as to have little or no time to dwell on her broken marriage, her hopes were fulfilled. She took over the choir from the recently retired "Mrs. Jenny Lee, (who) did beautiful work" and also had "about fifty piano students." In her work with the choir, she continued a tradition that had been very important to her father: "he insisted on them always singing spirituals."

But in 1931 the indecisive Dawson was finally persuaded to come to Tuskegee. Thereafter he and he alone directed the choir and all its activities, and Portia says that she only "filled in for him every now and then." It seems that there were some clashes between Portia and Dawson, whose behavior she describes as "so great and grand."

The black composer and arranger may have been overcompensating somewhat for his reactions to a situation he found difficult to negotiate. He had been brought in to lead Tuskegee's Music Department over the head of a woman who was his senior both in age and job tenure and who was the daughter of the school's founder to boot. Under these circumstances, though Portia says, "he was my boss and we did not get along," it is impossible not to feel some sympathy for him.

On one occasion, the great black composer W.C. Handy visited Tuskegee, and Portia told him that she would have the choir sing his arrangement of the spiritual "Give Me Jesus." Dawson, however, would not go along with her plans, making it clear that he considered Handy's blues-flavored version beneath the dignity of "his" singers.

But, professonal disagreements aside, even Portia had to admit that Moton's persistence in wooing Dawson away from Chicago had been justified. He soon raised the choir to national prominence, with tour appearances including one in 1932 at Radio City Music Hall in New York. In addition, his presence at Tuskegee attracted others to the school; he "beefed up" the faculty with important black musicians and composers and also invited major musical figures to perform and lecture.

A highlight of Portia's years at Tuskegee came when she was accompanist for Joseph Douglass. The noted black violinist, grandson of the great black leader and statesman Frederick Douglass (of whom she says "I remember sitting in his lap as a little girl" and "(my father) got a lot of inspiration from him"), gave a concert at Tuskegee a few years before his death in 1935.

Portia was pleased, too, when "all these celebrities (were at Tuskegee), to teach...those poor little kids," for two of them brought her the chance to renew old friendships and so make a reunion with her past. Dawson "had Abbie (Mitchell) come down to teach voice. And Hazel Harrison taught piano."

In the years since the early part of the century, when she preceded Portia at 58 Steglitzerstrasse in Berlin, Hazel Lucille Harrison had made a brilliant career, concertising to acclaim all over the United States and Europe after continuing her studies on both continents under such renowned teachers as Egon Petri and his master, the even more eminent Percy Grainger in Chicago, where he had settled in 1915. (Grainger was only one of many who predicted a great future for her, saying that she would someday "be at the top," where a place awaited her.)

Soon after coming to Tuskegee, Hazel became what Portia still fondly remembers as "the best friend I ever had." The times the two women spent together quickly developed into a specially vitalizing relationship that both of them could draw upon, and that would last through the years. Of Hazel's death in 1969, Portia says "I just thought it was the end of the world," and she adds with pride that she had "the privilege of speaking at her funeral at Howard."

Portia also says of her friend that "she did not teach regularly until Dawson had her come to Tuskegee." Once there, however, she began imparting to her students some of her excellent keyboard techniques and—more important—whatever she could of her own unerring sensitivity for music itself and the feelings it could convey. It was particularly fitting that Hazel Harrison's roster of pupils at this time included Fannie Virginia Pittman.

Despite her devotion to the work that took so much of her time and attention, and that was granting her a measure of equanimity vis-a-vis her former life, Portia was still very much concerned with her daughter's future. Though "Fannie (had) never really been well, she was a gifted little thing," whose love of music probably owed as much to her mother as to the fact that "Hazel Harrison was her teacher for years." Discussing her daughter's musical development, Portia again confesses some puzzlement. "(Hazel) was classical, too," but nevertheless Fannie "played all that stuff, ...I could never stand it." "That stuff," of course, was jazz, and in an effort to find a rationale for her uniquely disparaging opinion of that art form, Portia concludes: "well, people did not make as much of jazz (then) as they do now. They have really dignified jazz."

Jazz or no jazz, Portia continues, "as soon as she got old enough...about sixteen...I took her to Detroit. We had a relative there, and...Tuskegee boys (who) were friends of my daddy, and I got them to kind of look after her while she went to the Detroit Conservatory." Portia at this time had what is perhaps the most typical—and most pardonable—of a mother's dreams: that her daughter should follow in her footsteps.

At first, it must have seemed that this dream would be realized, for after Fannie's admission to the Detroit Conservatory of Music in 1934, she made good progress and "won a medal after she had been there one year and gave a recital with another girl." She won other awards as a student, and apparently did well enough to win a partial scholarship, but it was not enough to defray the costs involved. Portia could not help much, out of her $132-a-month paycheck, so Fannie went to work: "My daughter used to play a great deal of popular music...to help pay her expenses through music school in Detroit. At night she would go out on the boat in Lake Michigan and play for the people."

Fannie also studied briefly at the prestigious Juilliard School of Music in New York, her time in the great metropolis spent under the watchful supervision of her cousin once removed, John Washington's daughter Gertrude. (Portia wanted to prevent Fannie's undue exposure to the myriad temptations and delights of New York.)

In spite of what Portia calls her daughter's "gift for improvising (something she maintains that she herself could "never" do, always having to "work very hard at (her) notes"), something eventually led Fannie away from the difficult path that must be followed by any dedicated classical musician. It may have been something in her personality, which Portia ascribes to inheritance from her grandfather Pittman, who was "evidently quite a character," or something in the nature of the times, but instead of pursuing her studies, she "played with several orchestras and was called "The Little Washington Girl.""

But Portia tells us (with just a suspicion of a sigh—both sad and understanding—in her voice), Fannie soon gave this up, too. In different circumstances, but as her mother had before her, "she came on back to Tuskegee and got married." Portia's memory may be playing her false, for Fannie was not married at Tuskegee. She and Leonard Mitchell—whom she had met in Washington, D.C.— eloped after a short acquaintance.

Whatever hopes Portia had that marriage might succeed where music had obviously failed in providing a secure, peaceful life for her daughter were also destined to be dashed. The young couple's marital adjustment was difficult at best, and Fannie had particular trouble with Leonard's sister, with whom her relationship was characterized by an especially unpleasant kind of feminine sniping. It was an inauspicious beginning, and Fannie and Leonard were divorced after a year of marriage.

By 1934, the Depression had settled on the United States, blanketing the country with the gloom of the jobless, displaced, and restless; with breadlines and soup kitchens. Franklin Roosevelt was half way through his first term as President, trying by concrete measures, such as the T.V.A. and C.C.C., to return the nation to a more viable economic footing, and by his speeches to instill a new stimulus in the tired and dispirited American people.

By 1934, too, Portia had passed the halfway mark of her life. For many people, the fiftieth birthday is a time for stock-taking; a kind of landmark from which they can at once survey their past and attempt to scan the future for what it may have to disclose. It she did anything of the kind or made any kind of reassessment of her life, it is something she has since forgotten—perhaps because she preferred to. Then she bore the still-raw wounds of her failed marriage, as well as a host of anxieties about her three grown children.

FIFTEEN

"I would like to have left a contribution for my children!"

At a time when Fannie's problems seemed to be multiplying, Portia had almost completely lost touch with her middle child. Indeed, all she had of him as the 1930's drew to a close were snatches of second-hand information.

Booker had advanced steadily as a jazzman after dropping out of high school in his senior year. He had played and toured with several of the best groups in the Southwest and then joined a band headed by Cab Calloway's sister Blanche, moving east and recording for Victor (the forerunner of today's giant RCA). For a time he had been a member of the Congo Knights, based in New York, and when the Knights were absorbed by the larger Lucky Millinder band and then booked for a summer of performances in Europe, he went with them.

Booker did not return to the United States after the European tour, electing instead to remain in Paris and become part of that city's lively jazz scene—then a magnet for American musicians hard put to find work at home. There he met and worked with a Brazilian pianist named Romeo Silva, and a year later, Booker went to Brazil as part of

Silva's band. He then joined a largely American group of "big band" caliber and moved to Buenos Aires, where he would work successfully through World War II.

As for Portia's older son, he had always contributed the least to her burdens, but now it seemed that he was not fulfilling the promise of his early years. The quiet William Sidney Pittman, Jr., had been a good student at Howard, excelling in Latin. When he graduated in 1931, he had expressed an interest in becoming a lawyer. He had not, however, continued his schooling in this direction, and had taken instead a clerical job with the Post Office in Washington. He lived in a bachelor apartment and read law on his own, achieving quite a reputation in his small circle of friends as "the man with the answers," whatever the problems.

In spite of these and her other concerns during this period, Portia remained the woman she had always been—someone whose basically direct, pragmatic approach to life owed a great deal to her father. More than she knew, perhaps, in her determination to get on with her life, she was her father's daughter, and as his had, her life consisted more and more of work.

There was little else she could have done. Hazel Harrison had left Tuskegee in 1935, accepting an invitation from Lula Vere Childers—the energetic head of Howard's Music Department—to join the faculty of that university. Though the two women still corresponded, the immediate, supportive friendship that had meant so much was now denied her. It is not surprising that if work was all there was, Portia decided to expend all her energies on it.

Those energies were considerable, and it was then that she retired from Tuskegee Institute, started her own music school for the Tuskegee community, and became the kind of teacher that was already rare—the kind who gave her students a special pride in technique and a love of perfection that could not be acquired overnight, and the kind who was unwilling to sacrifice a solid foundation for quick, flashy results. Then as now, she could say, "I pride myself on knowing how to teach the fundamentals of piano, because most Americans today do not do it. They rush them too fast."

Portia's refusal to "rush" her pupils was clearly a carryover from her own student days in Berlin—she knew from experience what good teaching should be, and the philosophy that had been instilled in her then had remained with her. The succinct comment made by Teresa

Carreno in those days was one she agreed with: "1. Master the fundamentals. 2. Know what to do. 3. Do it."

The dedication she brought to her work caused her more conflict with William Dawson, and with their members of Tuskegee music department as well—even though she was no longer one of them. At one time their petty jealousies even gave rise to unpleasant rumors that she was undercutting the school by taking on her private students at rates considerably lower than those set by the department.

Notwithstanding such minor upsets, Tuskegee on the whole still afforded Portia a measure of security, a peaceful haven from the larger eruptions of life. This was true even after September 1, 1939, when the armed might of Nazi Germany smashed across the Polish border, bringing to an end futile years of what to some had been honorable negotiation; and to others, crawling appeasement.

But the American entry into the Second World War, after the Japanese attack on Pearl Harbor, was another matter. Now the upheavals that were shaking the larger world penetrated even as far as the comparative back-water that was Tuskegee, and their reverberations reached out in to Portia's life—for no one could remain completely untouched.

In common with countless thousands of other mothers around the world, Portia sent a son to war. William Sidney Pittman, Jr., inducted into the Army (in October, 1942), had become a cargo checker, serving in that capacity in North Africa, Italy, and Southern France. By the time of his discharge in 1945, he had been promoted to the rank of sergeant and had received various minor decorations and citations, including the Good Conduct Medal and the Meritorious Unit Award.

The war also involved Portia in a different way. A few days after her son's induction into military service, a small article appeared in the *New York Times*, announcing a forthcoming ship-launching in California. The craft that slid down the ways of the Wilmington shipyards in Los Angeles on September 29, 1942, was only one of eighteen "liberty ships" commissioned by the U.S. merchant marine in the course of World War II that bore the names of American Negroes. As the traditional bottle of champagne was smashed across her prow, she was christened the *Booker T. Washington*.

The 10,500-ton freighter was listed in the Lloyd's *Register of Ships* as belonging to the U.S. Department of Commerce, and as having a length of some 423 feet and a breadth of 57 feet. She had

81

been built by black labor, and on her maiden voyage, her integrated, international crew was commanded by Captain Hugh Mulzac, then the only black man who held a United States Masters Certificate.

According to the piece in the next day's *Times* describing the event, Marian Anderson performed the actual christening; Mary McLeod Bethune, then a director of the National Youth Administration, spoke; and Portia W. Pittman was on the guest list.

Precisely why Portia was merely an invited guest instead of a principal speaker is not clear—oddly enough, her existence may not have come to the attention of the committee in charge until the arrangements were nearly complete. She did attend the ceremonies, however, accompanied by her daughter (shortly before Fannie's second venture into marriage—with a violinist named Allen Lane—who took her to Chicago). Fannie's cousin Louise, Dave's daughter, was also there.

Portia does not recall Mrs. Bethune's being at the event, but her presence was a fitting one, because she had always credited Booker T. with having been a major formative influence on her life. Portia agrees that her father "gave Mrs. Bethune so much help," and that his philosophies had, to a large extent, shaped hers: "It is remarkable how closely her ideas about education coincided with those of my father." The two educators had faced and overcome similar obstacles along their paths to leadership, and Booker T's approval of her work in establishing Bethune-Cookson College in Daytona Beach, Florida, had meant a great deal to her.

The launching over, Portia returned to her quiet life at Tuskegee. By 1945, Fannie had joined her there, her second marriage, too, having ended in divorce. Once again, her relationship with her husband had been marked by in-law troubles; this time, Lane's attitude toward his mother had been a primary source of dissension. She now assisted Portia with her teaching and in general acted as her mother's helpmate.

V-E Day and V-J Day came and went, signalling the coming of peace at last to a war-weary world. In November, 1945, William Sidney Pittman, Jr., returned to the United States—one of the soldiers fortunate enough to have come through the war unwounded. That Portia's first child had come home a whole man was something to be deeply grateful for. So, in her sixty-third year, was the relatively placid life she had made for herself.

But despite her age and wishes at the time, the life of Booker T's child was about to enter a new and much more active phase. Instead of taking a back seat, she would once more become her father's daughter—and his principal spokeswoman.

SIXTEEN

I will allow no man, white or black, from the North or South, to drag me down so low that I will hate him."

The Hall of Fame for Great Americans was established at the turn of the century, based on a proposal by Henry M. MacCracken—then Chancellor of New York University—that the United States should honor its men of towering achievement as European nations did theirs. When the first election was held in 1900, twenty-nine men were chosen, representing a wide range of fields of endeavor. They included artist Gilbert Stuart, inventors Samuel F.B. Morse and Eli Whitney, authors Nathaniel Hawthorne and Washington Irving, statesmen Benjamin Franklin and Daniel Webster, and military leaders Admiral David Farragut and Robert E. Lee. Five presidents of the United States were also elected—John Adams, Thomas Jefferson, Abraham Lincoln, Ulysses Grant, and, of course, George Washington.

Elections were held every five years thereafter, with the slate of names of prospective candidates each time submitted for final selection to the New York University Senate. This body also chose the artists who sculped the bronze busts to be placed in the colon-naded Hall of Fame itself, on the University's Bronx campus.

In November, 1945, Booker T. Washington was elected to the Hall of Fame (along with Revolutionary War leader Tom Paine, southern poet and composer Sidney Lanier, and U.S. Army doctor Walter Reed, whose work had been instrumental in contolling yellow fever). His thus became the only black name among these seventy-

84

seven in the Hall of Fame, and the subsequent commission of black sculptor Richmond Barthe to create the bust of Booker T. added another "first" to the Hall's history. (The bust was a joint gift by Tuskegee and Hampton Institutes.)

Then, on Thursday, May 23, 1946, at N.Y.U.'s Gould Memorial Library, Portia (escorted by her son, newly "separated" from the Army) stood proudly as the Tuskegee choir, led by William Dawson, sang the National Anthem and several of her father's favorite spirituals. When her eighteen-year-old niece Gloria (another of Dave's four daughters) unveiled the bronze bust, Portia was not the only guest who was moved to tears. And when she reverently received from Gloria's hands the grey felt cloth that had covered it, it was one of the most memorable moments in her life.

Tributes on the occasion poured in from all over the country, but perhaps the most fitting—and the simplest—came from President Harry S. Truman! "He was a great American....His rise is in the great American tradition of advancement by industry, patience, and perseverance."

The next day, when the bust was placed in the niche prepared for it in the Hall of Fame, Portia and Sidney were again among the onlookers. She told an interviewer at the time that it had been her belief in God "and faith alone" that had brought her to that high point, where she could see "all the wonderful things that were happening to Booker T's memory." Other things had indeed been happening, and she had been part of them almost from their inception. Within a few years, however, Portia would have reason to question just how "wonderful" they were; and because of them, she would be in greater need than ever of the sustenance her faith could give her.

She had first encountered the energetic Sidney J. Phillips at Tuskegee, when he was a member of the Agricultural Department. (He had also been involved in advertising, for a soft drink concern.) The end of the war found him in Washington, where he had been working with the Interior and Commerce Departments.

Portia may never have known exactly when and how the idea of making a national memorial of her father's Virginia birthplace began to take shape in Phillips' mind, but by the time Booker T. was enshrined in the Hall of Fame, his brainchild was practically full-grown. As self-designated president of the Booker T. Washington Memorial Foundation, he had used his governmental connections to good advantage, and the plan was virtually barrelling down the path to

realization. Funds had been raised to buy what was left of the Burroughs plantation (the slave cabins themselves were long gone) from
its owners, and the site had acquired a state charter. Presidential and
Congressional approval came quickly, and what would have been
Booker T's ninetieth birthday saw the special issue of 5,000,000 half-
dollars, bearing his likeness, by the United States Mints in Philadelphia, Denver, and San Francisco. The coins were to be sold for
$1.00 each, the profits to go to the foundation for its work in restoring
the plantation, and setting up a vocational school on the site, toward
its scholarship fund for needy black students, and to pay for upkeep
and the salaries of the office workers needed to run these various
enterprises.

Much of Phillips' initial success was due—in addition to his own
not inconsiderable powers of persuasion—to Portia, whom he had
made the foundation's living symbols. She first visited the site in
1946, saying of it "I felt deeply thrilled. I felt as though I really
belonged up there," and in 1947, she had even moved to Washington—giving up her music school at Tuskegee—in order to be in closer
touch with the focus of its activities. She says now that she "helped
him raise a lot of money" with her "running around." At any rate,
newspaper articles began to appear around the country, showing
Portia with a beaming Harry S. Truman (with whose musical daughter Margaret she had something in common, and who once went so far
as to make sure that Fannie was not left out of camera range for a
group photograph, saying "she's her own flesh and blood"; with
Alben Barkley, the charming "Veep" who had a carefully cultivated
reputation as a bon vivant and ladies man; and with countless other
dignitaries. Traveling nationwide, Portia addressed civic groups,
autographed copies of *Up From Slavery*, gave interviews, and did
whatever Phillips asked of her to raise money for the project. Phillips
had been equally successful in roping other Washingtons into his
scheme, and at the memorial's groundbreaking ceremonies on April
12, 1946, Booker T's great-grandson, Booker T. Washington III,
was photographed turning over the first shovelful of dirt. (Later in life,
he would become an almost-recluse, giving such—and indeed any—
activities connected with his famous name a wide berth.)

Surface progress nowithstanding, by 1951, when Congress
authorized a second half-dollar—this one commemorating both
Booker T. and George Washington Carver (the profits from both
issues eventually reached $75,000)—the foundation had already run

into difficulties. In spite of all of Phillips' "huckstering" efforts, which included a syndicated column featured in many American newspapers, there had been trouble. Much of it had arisen in Congress, over his proposal to erect a large hospital for black veterans on the memorial site. Even though Portia had been trotted out to testify in its behalf before the House Veterans Committee, and even though Phillips himself had spoken to the committee members, saying that he "had no objection to segregation," others did register their opposition. The hospital bill was attacked as "Jim Crow" legislation on the floor of Congress, its opponents including representatives Adam Clayton Powell and Jacob Javits (then in his second term in Congress). The bill was defeated and the hospital was never built.

This reversal had brought the whole memorial a good deal of unfavorable publicity, and then, two days before Christmas, 1951, it was dealt another blow, in the form of a fire that caused over $100,000 in damages. But Phillips' determination did not go up in smoke, and, though Portia had begun to have some second thoughts about her involvement in the project, for the sake of her father's memory, she continued her work with him.

In the next few years, they had several minor successes, including the renaming—in 1953—of Virginia's state highway 122, which ran past the site, as the Booker T. Washington Memorial Highway. But Portia had already become a less docile performer, and she soon came to feel that Phillips was far from what he seemed. By 1953, too, matters had reached a point at which her questions could no longer be stilled, and she sued him for $20,000 in a Washington, D.C. district court, alleging that he had reneged on a contract they had made by which she was to get $25,000—to be paid over a five-year period—from the coins issued in 1951. All she had ever received, she said, was the original payment of $3,000 stipulated in the document. A co-suit against Phillips was brought by Robert Ephraim, a young man who was listed as the secretary of Booker T. Washington Foundation that Portia herself had set up—as much for her own protection as to perpetuate her father's name. Both lawsuits proved futile, for Phillips took refuge in claims that the foundation was a non-profit foundation, and that all of its funds had gone into its good works, not the least of which was the $20,000 yearly salary he had paid himself.

While Portia was still embroiled in litigation, others had also become suspicious of Phillips and his methods of running the foundation. The outcries against him grew louder and louder, especially in the black press. He had never deemed it necessary to make any public accounting of his disposition of funds, and it was widely said that his efforts had done more for his own self-aggrandizement than for the avowed goals of the foundation. Phillips used his newspaper column to protest the allegations aginst him, making counterattacks of his own, including the comment—remarkable for a man in his tenuous position—that it was "always news" when Negroes "met their responsibilities in community work."

Within a year, the 100th anniversary of Booker T's birth would be celebrated. The foundation owed almost $100,000 for promotional campaigns alone and had other oustanding debts totaling half as much again. Phillips was being blamed for his "overconfidence of success," but it seemed to Portia that one of her brightest dreams had also reached a sorry nadir. Nevertheless, when the memorial had to be sold at auction, she still did all she could to rescue at least part of that dream—even to the point of becoming a contestant on a television quiz show and going to Phillips' friends to raise the $16,000 it took to purchase the site.

But there were others who were aware of the the approaching centennial, and others who felt that Booker T's memory was being poorly served. One of them was California Representative Clair Engle, who introduced a bill in the House providing for the United

The house in Virginia where Booker T. was born (still standing).

States to purchase the birthplace. The bill was passed by Congress, and on April 2, 1956, President Dwight D. Eisenhower signed Public Law 464, securing the memorial's future at last. Portia expressed her joy that she had lived to see "such an honor bestowed upon [her father] by a grateful nation," and some months later, when she paid a courtesy call on "Ike" at the White House, she assured him of her support in the upcoming election. (Congress also appropriated $225,000 to celebrate the centennial, and $14,000,000 worth of centennial stamps were issued on the day itself.)

On June 18, 1957, the Booker T. Washington Memorial became the Booker T. Washington National Monument, administered by the National Parks Service. In his official statement on taking possession of the 218-acre site, Secretary of Interior Fred A. Seaton (the Parks Service is part of the Interior Department) described Booker T. as "a man whose ideals have left an indelible imprint, and whose life established for his race a pattern of advancement founded on the basic virtues of industry, thrift, and racial harmony."

Thus what Portia justifiably felt to be the crowning achievement of her life came as she neared her seventy-fifth birthday. If she had wanted to—but was never given to such backward glances—she could have looked at her almost-completed three-quarters of a century and seen a picture that—though it contained some darker or indistinct areas—was overwhelmingly a bright one.

William Sidney Pittman had died that year in Dallas, bringing to a close that unhappy chapter in her life. She had never seen him again or communicated with him after their separation, but she had made sure—out of her unfailing sense of what was right—that her children remained in touch with their father, at least as long as she had any say in the matter. In 1954 the oldest of those children had retired from the Postal Service, receiving a certificate of recognition from the postmaster general honoring him for his devotion to duty during his career there. And Fannie had married again; with her third husband Dr. Alonzo Marcelle Kennedy (a quiet, understanding physician twenty-one years her senior) she had found some of the stability she had always sought, and the "veil" Portia says covered her face at birth had apparently lifted. Portia had happy memories of her visits with the couple in their comfortable Kansas City home.

Portia was still doing some work for her own foundation, most of it in the scholarship area. One of the recipients was her grand-nephew, the son of Booker T. Washington III. Through a former Bradford classmate, she obtained a place for little "Larry"—Lawrence Booker in the High Mowing School, in Wilmot, New Hampshire. The principal of what Portia calls "this rather unique school," Mrs. Beulah Emick, had also taken several other black pupils on Portia's recommendation. Besides such efforts, however, it had become time—even for her—to wind down, to move at a somewhat slower pace, She was still taking life in both hands, but more gently than before, and when Fannie had asked her to come live with her and Dr. Kennedy in Kansas, she had accepted—it would be good for all concerned.

So it was that she (and Fannie) had to travel to New York for the filling-in of the largest blank space in her life. In 1962, Portia was reunited with her second son. His own life for the past thirty years had been anything but an easy one.

At the end of the Second World War, Booker had left Argentina for Brazil, where he continued to play with hotel and especially casino orchestras for several years. But he had grown dissatisfied with the kind of music audiences seemed to want, and after 1950, when gambling was outlawed in Brazil, had found it increasingly difficult to get work. He dropped out, stopped all communication with his family in the United States, and virtually disappeared. Rumors even reached his mother that he had died, but, she says, "I never believed that Booker was dead. I felt something was wrong, but I didn't know what."   . . .

Her feeling was later proved to be an instance of infallible mother's instinct. There *had* been something, and it had been that most regrettable part of the international music scene—drugs and alcohol. His involvement with them had grown so deep that at one time he collapsed on stage during an engagement, and, as he later told his mother, "The truth is, Momma, I died twice."

The curious agent of Booker T. Pittmans' resurrection had been a French travelling salesman. One of his frequent trips into the Brazilian interior had taken him to a small coffee town in the state of Parana, called Sao Antonia da Platina. There, Portia continues, Philippe de Corcodel—was also a jazz bugg—went to a nightclub to while away a few hours and had an unexpectedly interesting evening. Portia tells us what happened:

Booker drank. He tried marijuana. He became very ill....he decided he was going to give it up. He went out in some old country town where he wasn't known. He said he went there to die but he kept on living....they asked him to sell his instruments that he cared too much for [but] he said he would rather die than sell them....[Though] he would not let that get away from him, he became very thin and his personality—it was not like him at all....One day he was in a little restaurant with his horn, playing one of his old tunes, and it seems that this French salesman...happened to be in there and he said 'My goodness, nobody else could ever play like that but Booker Pittman and Booker Pittman is dead.'

On his return to Rio, Corcodel's announcement of his discovery produced such disbelief that he had to return to Sao Antonio da Platina and take pictures and tapes of Booker to prove his story was true. After that, Portia says, he "persuaded him to come back into the music world, and oh! from then on he was a sensation."

Booker had other help on his way back into the world he had left nearly ten years before, and Portia seems to feel that perhaps he was a little too grateful (again, a typically maternal reaction on her part— especially since she had had seen so very little of his son):

I think he felt deeply obligated to...this woman Ofelia, who helped to bring him back to health. She was working in some theater there and Louis Armstrong's band was playing—they were great friends—and she made Louis take an interest in him. She brought him back to himself better than anyone else. So as a result of that he felt that he owed his life to her and that is why he gave this girl Eliana, his stepdaughter, so much prestige. If it wasn't for Booker, she wouldn't have come on as fast as she did.

Booker had become a jazz star again, much to the delight of South American jazz-lovers, who felt he would become their version of Sidney Bechet. He was featured in Brazilian and Argentine clubs and on television; received rave reviews for his appearances, and was cutting a number of records.

In 1959 he had married the attractive, widowed Ofelia whom he had first met in Satchmo's Rio dressing room. She had become his manager and agent, and he had developed a good relationship with her young daughter, Eliana. By 1962, when he brought his family to the United States to attend a jazz festival and for his reunion with his mother, the seventeen-year-old Eliana (who was usually described as a beautiful young woman but whom Portia chooses to remember as "very pretty") had started on a musical career of her own.

Portia says that her son was largely responsible for his stepdaughter's success, that he "helped her with her lyrics, language, and in every way...stood right behind her." Booker also did well on his return to his native land, numbering recording and club dates as well as TV shots among his appearances. He was treated as a giant from the jazz past, feted, praised, and eagerly listened to and quoted. In one interview, Booker said that though he liked many of the current jazz stars such as Miles Davis and John Coltrane, he believed that jazz should "never lose touch with its roots, its sense of the past."

As a comeback, it was all Portia—or anyone—could have wished for, but it was destined to be blighted, for Booker often returned to Brazil, and his past caught up with him. The years in the hinterlands, which he had spent "drinking rum" and living what he called "the good life" had undermined his health. Portia still cannot speak of her young son's death without pain:

After he died down there, they found out that he had lost his voice for about a year. I didn't know he was so ill, or I would have made the State department send me over to see about him...he got so he couldn't talk and he didn't want me to know about it.

When Booker T. Pittman died—a victim of cancer—in a Sao Paulo hospital in October, 1969, it meant that of Portia's three children, only Fannie was left to her. William Sidney Pittman, Jr., had died in 1967; after some four years spent fighting a variety of ailments, ranging from gastric disturbances to severe arthritis, he was not strong enough to recover from a fall in which he broke his hip.

At the age of eighty, Portia had left her home with the Kennedys to be with her "oldest boy." Some of the letters she wrote him before her return to Washington contain clues to what she gave up, and to why she always speaks of the years in Kansas City as "very restful for me." It was a time spent on a peaceful plateau, far—but not too far—from the world's troubles:

...Mr. Phillips called me two weeks ago and said he wanted my opinion about a letter he had written Gov. Barnett [Mississippi's] Governor Ross Barnett, who had just failed to outface Deputy Attorney Genral Nicholas Katzenbach and a veritable army of federal marshals over James Meredith's enrollment in the University of Mississippi and wanted a written reply from me—and said he would enclose a small check—so far, no letter and no check. I am very suspicious of him when it comes to this, as you know. No one could respect that Governor. But I admire Meredith for sticking it out....We have a very comfortable place to live—the weather is fine....

The rest of the letter deals with another aspect of the news. Even as a little girl Portia had liked baseball, and now her interest in the "Great American Sport" continued unabated. It was one her daughter shared: "Fannie was sick about the Yankies winning. She had pulled so hard for the Giants." (The New York team had just squeaked past their San Francisco opponents in a 4-3 cliffhanger World Series.)

A few weeks later, she wrote her son again:

"We are well and happy. Marcelle feeds me so much that I am having a hard time with my poundage.

"The world conditions are very complicated, and I do wish we could talk things over as we used to do. It looks as tho [sic] brother Castro is causing a bit of uneasiness, and how about "Old Miss" and the U.S. Justice Department—I do hope they indict Gov. Barnett and all the others implicated. You should have been with me to hear Martin L. King last Sunday. The auditorium was packed—white and colored, and did he speak!

"....I am beginning to like this place better. For one thing I am not bothered with many low down gossiping Negroes. They were so mean and jealous of me in Washington, altho I had many fine true friends whom I shall always contact....Please let me know how things are with you. Would you like to visit me sometime if I can make the arrangements?... [Marcelle] is very kind to me, and it is so nice not to have people cursing and calling you names...."

But by January, 1963, Sidney was in Washington's Mount Alto Veteran's Hospital, and Portia had cause for concern: "The doctors seem to feel that you will be confined a long time. The V.A. office said their only fear was they you would try to get out. Please wait until you are cured and pray for parience." In March, when she wrote him again, she said he had been informed that his condition was satisfactory, but she herself was recovering from a bout with "this dreadful flue [sic]."

After Sidney's death, the life that Portia lived with her daughter (for Fannie had come to Washington to be with her, returning to Kansas city only in 1968, to supervise Dr. Kennedy's funeral arrangements) was a quiet one, growing increasingly lonely because, like many of those who survive into real old age, she found herself in a position in which the obituary pages of the daily newspapers had become something to be avoided—the names listed there always seemed to include some one that she knew. As Portia says now, so many among her family and friends had "left [her] here with a memory."

Her memories, however, were good ones, and if the needle charting the beat of her life drew a fairly even line, it also recorded some peaks. There was a renewal of her friendship with Hazel Harrison, who spent her last years in a Washington nursing home, and the two former Tuskegee music teachers had had a small reunion with the head of their department, William Dawson, by then also retired, when he "had us out to dinner at one of the hotels downtown." At the time, Portia says, "Hazel could hardly walk, poor thing," and she died shortly afterward, in April, 1969. When Portia addressed the mourners assembled for Hazel's funeral services in the Howard University Chapel, she spoke without notes. She needed no written reminders, for her words came from the heart of friendship.

There had been others who sought her out in those quiet years— she had been an honored guest at Tuskegee's eighty-fifth anniversary dinner at the Waldorf-Astoria in New York, and was photographed with trustee General Lucius D. Clay after his speech on the occasion. She had cut the ribbon at the dedication of a new visitors' center at the Booker T. Washington National Monument—ten years to the day after she had participated in the original dedication ceremonies of the birthplace. And about a month before her eighty-seventh birthday, she paid a return visit to the White House, to have lunch with Robert Brown—one of Richard Nixon's special assistants. She and Brown (then one of the highest-ranking blacks in the Nixon administration) discussed the racial situation and the President's efforts toward school desegregation, which Portia believed he was handling "in a very sensible way." She also recalled for reporters her first visit to the executive mansion, shortly after her marriage to Pittman. Then the bluff, direct Teddy Roosevelt had given them his typical greeting of "I'm bully glad to see you," shown them around, and given them each a small gift as a memento of the meeting. Another connection with Roosevelt had lasted as well—Portia and T.R.'s daughter, the widowed Alice Roosevelt Longworth, still saw each other occasionally, and Portia's flood of birthday messages that year included a call from Mrs. Longworth; at eighty-seven herself, she was as outspoken as she had ever been.

Roy L. Hill with Portia, and large "87th" birthday cake.

It was on her eighty-seventh birthday, too—before he days-long and all-night celebrations—that she told a journalist who had asked her to comment on her longevity, "I guess I am living out my father's years." That remark contained more wisdom than wit, and more self-knowledge than sarcasm; in those few simple words, Portia had expressed the essential truth of what being Booker T's child had meant to her.

Booker Taliaferro Washington as a young man.

SEVENTEEN

"He was a universal man."

A sense of having outlived one's times is probably the saddest bond shared by the very old, no matter how untouched they are by the physical and mental infirmities of the advancing years. It is perhaps especially those who have not been anesthetized by senility—whose senses have not been dulled and who try hardest to stay in touch with what is current—who find themnselves the most disoriented and sorely tried. To them, the young seem strangely unwilling to benefit by their experiences, oddly unprepared to learn the many lessons life has to teach. Indeed, those who are the future often go further in their readiness to criticize and find fault, making of years of hard-won wisdom an accusation instead of a praiseworthy accomplishment. Portia knows this—and she know the young—so a special awareness always hovers just below the surface of her speech, ready to break through whenever she discusses her life:

Sometimes they claim that I don't associate with those in my class, but I find so many good things in people that never had the opportunities that I had. I find them interesting and I learn from them. I think that is one characteristic I take from my father.

96

If it is words like "class," "opportunities," and "interesting" that are often thrown up to Portia, they also lay at the heart of her father's problems. She knows this, too, and carries within her the realization that the life he made for her was responsible:

I met so many people during my childhood days....this was a great advantage, and it influenced my life. I sometimes think, though, that [because of] being away from my own race it took me a long time to adjust myself. [was] coming back into a new world, as it was.... Our people had different ideas and different ways of living and I had to get used to that. It was kind of hard. It was hard for a girl who had been reared under such an environment, a New England culture—people so sweet and so kind and so different—and then suddenly to be plunged into another [world]. There was an undercurrent of jealousy on their part—my father had to fight this all his life.

Whether he fought it or "didn't pay any attention to it"—as she later said—Booker T. had also a lot to "get used to." Portia's disorientation was involuntary, but his had come about through his own choice. His work had turned him into a kind of circus performer, a juggler on a tightrope who had to balance two often opposing viewpoints—the expectations of the white world in which he usually moved and those of his own people, for whose sake he did so. Such statements as "race, like crabs, pulls a man down" (which Portia elaborates as meaning "one gets up a little and others are pulling him and one another down") and "a good many colored folk that try to be white find that it isn't as pleasant as they imagined it would be....white folks don't really have a good time, from the Negro point of view" show how very delicate a position his was.

Its delicacy was compounded by a third factor—his own wishes and drives. It had been these, as much as anything else, that had let to his establishing Tuskegee in the first place. Though the "uses of power" never became for him an end in themselves, he certainly was enough of a pragmatist so that, as his daughter says, "power was his game and he used ideas as instruments...."

"His game" led him to assume disguises, and chameleon-like, he became whatever "they" wanted him to be, as excerpts from a speech he made before the Wisconsin state legislature in March, 1911, illustrate:

. . .

A careful census of Negroes who have been graduated from the

97

The Booker T. Washington monument, "lifting the veil" (at Tuskegee).

institute has failed to reveal the name of any man or woman who has been sentenced to prison or who has been elected to a state legislature.

A nicely ironic witticism, and Booker T. could not have known that, years later, it would retroactively be given the lie by his own son-in-law. But he did know how to be a crowd-pleaser, and he continued with more remarks carefully calculated to charm his Northern audience, explaining that spiritualism had failed to catch on at Tuskegee because it had little practical value:

...the spirits come only at night and they...confine their activities to such things as moving a table leg, tapping a piano key, or making a few marks on some paper. Now, if they could be made to get up at five o'clock in the morning, build the fire, prepare breakfast and set it on the table, or could be made to plow the fields in the spring, mow the corn, tend and harvest it in the fall, we would all be spiritualists.

Such humor pleased the legislators, as it was meant to. It made him seem trustworthy, and if it also led to some of his own people regarding him as an "Uncle Tom" or a "white nigger," that was something he had learned to take into account. As Louis Harlan, editor of the Booker T. Washington papers, put it:

"...he usually could not choose between a wide range of public positions, and if he wanted to reach a goal which he shared with other Negroes but of which whites would disapprove, he had to...move toward the goal at some level of privacy or secrecy....He did it in his own way rather than in the way some other men a thousand miles or seventy years away would have had him do it."

There were others, closer than a thousand miles, and nearer than seventy years. If Ralph Ellison, whose *Invisible Man* contains what Portia calls "things about Tuskegee I didn't want to know," described Booker T. in his novel as a man who was "strong enough to choose to do the wise thing in spite of what he felt himself," some men in his own time found his rope-dancing hard to equate with their ideas of how the progress of the race should best be achieved.

One of them was W.E.B. DuBois, and his and Booker T's ideas were effectively summed up in Dudley Randall's poem, "Booker T. and W.E.B.:*

"It seems to me, said Booker T.,
"I shows a mighty lot of cheek
To study chemistry and Greek
When Mister Charlie needs a hand
To hoe the cotton on his land,
And when Miss Ann looks for a cook,
Why stick your nose inside a book?"

"I don't agree," said W.E.B.,
"If I should have the drive to seek
Knowledge of chemistry or Greek,
I'll do it. Charles and Miss can look
Another place for hand or cook,
Some men rejoice in skill of hand,
And some in cultivating land,
But there are others who maintain
The right to cultivate the brain."

*Louis R. Harlan and Pete Daniel, "A Dark and Stormy Night in the Life of Booker T. Washington," *Graduate School Chronicle,* University of Maryland. 1970, 111:2, p. 7.

"It seems to me," said Booker T.,
"That all you folks have missed the boat
Who shout about the right to vote,
And spend vain days and sleepless nights
In uproar over civil rights.
Just keep your mouths shut, do not grouse,
But work, and save, and buy a house."

"I don't agree," said W.E.B.,
"For what can property avail
If dignity and justice fail.
Unless you help to make the laws,
They'll steal your house with a trumped-up clause.
A rope's as tight, a fire as hot,
No matter how much cash you've got.
Speak soft, and try your little plan,
But as for me, I'll be a man."

"It seems to me," said Booker T.—

"I don't agree,"
Said W.E.B.

In his early days in the forefront of the Niagara Movement, which later became the NAACP, DuBois had been one of those most strongly opposed to Booker T. (Poet Paul Laurence Dunbar had also attacked Tuskegee's premise of industrial training, as early as 1898, saying that it seemed to "imply [that the Negro] should not work with his head.") By the time he became director of publications and research for that organization, however, he was readier to submerge his disagreements in the general striving for equality, and in 1932, Portia tells us, he in effect admitted that her father had been right.

Our ideas and responses are all part of a chain reaction, for we are invisibly linked to the times and ideas of our parents, and their parents, going farther back than we are able—or indeed willing—to see. So Portia's ideas about the present structure of race relations in the United States are a product of her times and of her father's—they could hardly be anything else:

"I am so happy today to realize that the NAACP has turned over a new leaf. You know, they organized to fight my father, his voice, his philosophy....just like these belligerent people now....

"What we want is nonviolence in equality when it comes to jobs and education and things of that kind, but if we are going to fight with force we might as well be black klansmen. See what I mean?

"When I say [I am] against force [I don't mean there aren't] times when one does have to get up on his haunches or stand squarely on his feet, too, because there are bullies who will absolutely try to walk all over you."

Speaking of some of the 1960's demonstrations, she says that her father's reaction would have been a practical one: "He would have said, 'don't go out in the street and wear your shoes out, go out and learn how to make them." But for herself, she adds, "it has just got to work both ways," and when black voter registration drives in Tuskegee initially moved at a slow pace, she approved of what happened next:

So what they did was to stop trade in the town. They cut out every white place of business and some had to close their stores and leave town because they could not make a living. The Negroes started to build stores, supermarkets, and dress shops, and all of that sort of thing that they should have been doing for years. When you bother a man's pocketbook, you change a little bit.

In spite of everything that has changed, Portia still believes that "there is so much ignorance on both sides," and she would agree that "despite the increased opportunity that has touched the lives of some blacks, America remains a dual society in which attitudes are shaped by a social reality that is at once bountiful and merciless, promising and perilous. To live with that reality is not easy." *As she has always been, so she remains—more than ready to learn and to make her contribution. And to those who doubt her right to do so, or who question the relevance of her more than ninety years of living to today's situation, she might reply that whether or not it was truly a black experience" is immaterial—it was hers.

°*The New York Times,* Monday, August 27, 1973, p. 1.

EIGHTEEN

"The devil didn't want me and God—well, he just isn't ready for me yet."

On Wednesday, June 6, 1973, Portia observed her ninetieth birthday. And if the celebration that marked the occasion was a bit quieter, a bit smaller in scope, than the party on her eighty-seventh, it was no less sparkling. (It was by far a happier day than the one she spent the year before. The eighty-eighth anniversary of her birth had passed almost unnoticed, because she was in the intensive-care unit of a Washington hospital recovering from a siege of heart-irregularity.)

There were reporters on this day, too, several of whom later commented that in many ways she still resembled a debutante far more than a woman of her years. In fact, she herself said, "I feel like I am sweet sixteen—and without a boyfriend!" and was frequently heard to complain that the members of the press had "rushed her so" that she had not had time to adjust her wig or finish her makeup to her satisfaction.

But she had no cause to grumble at the pictures that appeared in the next day's papers, showing her in a rose-pink suit (she had given up her struggle with the wig by then), graced by a white corsage. Knife in hand, she was poised to cut into a large chocolate cake, elaborately festooned with confectionery swirls and topped by a mound of butter-cream roses.

There was enough cake for the roomful of guests, and after the assembled relatives and friends had raised their glasses of punch in salute, a voice called out, "Go on, Aunt Portia, make a wish! Now, cut!

No gathering at Portia's would have been complete without music, and as the rich, cascading tones of a tenor saxophone came from the tape recorder, she said to her daughter, "That sounds like my Booker. No one else ever put so much feeling into jazz." "It is, Ma," Fannie replied. "It's a tape I made from some of his records." There were reminiscences, then, for Portia, in the course of which she came to some conclusions about her life:

Being the daughter of a great man has had its ups and down, but I would rather be the poor daughter of Booker T. Washington than the rich daughter of the wealthiest man on earth.

Later, she admitted to having been "a little tired" before her party, but she had been stimulated by the warm glow of comfortable conversation and good feelings it had engendered. In the pop of flash-bulbs and shouts of "Happy Birthday" earlier, no one had thought to ask Portia about her wish. She, at least, had no doubts as to its coming true: in her vibrant, slightly breathy voice—as full as ever of her enthusiasm for life—she summed up the day with a remark that (with no qualifications whatsoever) could have stood for the ninety years she had just completed:

"I have always known how to make a little magic. That is what it is all about."

Clockwise from Upper Left: A/Mrs. Fannie Washington (Portia's mother).
B/Amanda Ferguson-Johnson (Booker T's sister). C/Booker T. Washington.
D/John Henry Washington (Booker T's older brother).

Clockwise, from Upper Left: A/Portia Washington while at Bradford College. B/Jane Ethel Clark (Portia's chaperone in Europe). C/Abbie Mitchell, Dramatic Soprano. D/Professor Martin Krause (Portia's piano teacher in Germany.

A

C

B

Clockwise from Upper Left: A/Left to Right-Booker T. II, Booker T., and E. Davidson Washington (second son). B/Margaret James Murray Washington (Booker T's third wife). C/Olivia A. Davidson Washington (Booker T's second wife).

107

Clockwise from Upper Left: A/Portia. B/Portia. C/Portia, with friends, including author Roy Hill. D/Left to Right-Joseph H. Douglass (son of Hailey Douglass), Nettie Washington Douglass. E/Portia.

A

B

A/Portia at piano, with Fannie (her daughter). B/Left to Right-Nettie Douglass (Mrs. Frederick Douglass, III), Fannie Howard Douglass (Mrs. Joseph H. Douglass) and Nettie Washington Douglass Morris; in background, the residence of Frederick Douglass in Washington, D.C.

109

A

B

C

Clockwise from Upper Left: A/Left to Right—William S. Pittman, Jr., Fannie Pittman, Booker T. Washington, Booker T., III, and Booker T. Pittman (Portia's son). B/Left to Right—William Sidney, Fannie Virginia Pittman (Portia's daughter), and Portia. C/Booker T., with favorite mount.

Clockwise from Upper Left: A/Left to Right-President Dwight D. Eisenhower and Portia. B/Vice President Albert Barkley of Kentucky and Portia. C/The Honorable Carl Albert, Oklahoma, Speaker of the House, with Portia holding a copy of Booker T's *Up from Slavery*. D/Left to Right-President Harry S. Truman, and document establishing Booker T. Washington Birth Place Park in Hale Ford, Virginia, with Portia, Fannie and assembled dignitaries.

A

C

B

Clockwise from Upper Left: A/Chapel (with the brick from Booker T's birthplace cabin). B/Booker T (on last visit to New York. C/The launching of the Liberty Ship: *The Booker T. Washington.*

112

A

C

B

Clockwise from Upper Left:A/The Oaks, the Booker T. Washington Home, Tuskegee Institute. B/Right to Left-Fannie, Frederick Douglass, III, Joseph H. Douglass and Blanche Elizabeth Douglass. C/The Family: William Sidney, Jr. (Portia's son), Portia, and Fannie.

A

C

B

Clockwise from Upper Left: A/Left to Right-Dr. Marcellus Kennedy, Fannie V. Kennedy, A. Phillip Randolph and Portia, at Fannie's wedding, Kansas City, Missouri. B/Portia, Booker T. Pittman, Fannie Kennedy. C/William Sidney Pittman (Fannie's groom).

114

A

C

B

Clockwise from Upper Left: A/Portia and daughter Fannie. B/Left to Right-Portia, Roy L. Hill, David E. Cabbiness (Portia's grand-nephew). C/Fannie Pittman Kennedy.

Clockwise from Upper Left: A/Left to Right-Ophelia Pittman, Booker T., and Eliana Pittman. B/Dr.. Lawrence "Larry" Washington and his bride (Dr. Pamela H. Washington). C/Left to Right-Dr. Harvey (President of Hampton University), Roy L. Hill, and Portia, greeting Dr. Frederick Patterson (third President of Tuskegee University).

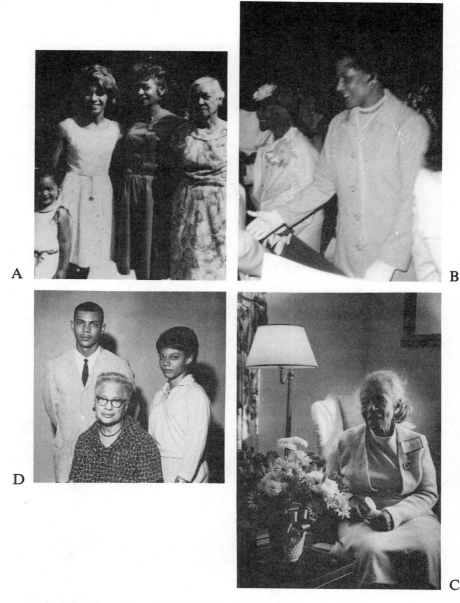

Clockwise from Upper Left: A/Left to Right-Nettie Morris, Nettie W. Douglass-Morris, Nettie Hancock Washington Douglass and Mrs. Nettie Hancock Washington. B/Mrs. Margaret E. Clifford (niece of Portia), at Tuskegee University, Founder's Day. C/Portia (at her 69th Class Reunion 1974, Bradford College). D/Mrs. Edith M. Washington and two of her grandchildren.

A/Portia, cake-time (birthday party, June 6, 1974).

B/Portia, Tuskegee's Founder's Day.

118

Clockwise from Upper Left: A/Robert Russa Moton (second President of Tuskegee University). B/Dr. Frederick D. Patterson (third President of Tuskegee University). C/Dr. Luther H. Foster (fourth President of Tuskegee University). D/Dr. Benjamin F. Payton (fifth President of Tuskegee University).

Clockwise from Upper Left: A/Booker T., Jr., record jacket and sax. B/S.M. Downs, music teacher of Portia's. C/Samuel Coleridge Taylor.

A Biographical Note on Booker T. Washington, Jr.

Booker Taliaferro Washington, Jr. (May 29, 1887 - February 5, 1945), originally given the name Baker in honor of his parents' benefactor, Eleanor Jamerson Williams Baker. After the death of his mother Olivia Davidson Washington, Booker T. Washington Jr. was placed under the care of Mrs. Dora S. King and other nurses at Tuskegee and in New England until Booker T. Washington's marriage to Margaret James Murry provided a more settled family life. Booker T. Washington Jr. attended the Tuskegee Institute practice school. In 1902 he entered Wellesley School for Boys in Wellesley, Mass. Edward Augustine Benner, its principal, was an admirer of Booker T. Washington, but he was one of a series of headmasters who were sorely tried by the son's schoolboy pranks, truancy, and fast motorcycle. Leaving Wellesley School in 1904, Booker T. Washington Jr. spent a year in school at Tuskegee and graduated. He then entered Dummer Academy in South Byfield, Mass. He dropped out briefly in 1905 to build up his physical health, but returned to Dummer until the spring of 1907.

During his last year at Dummer Academy, Booker T. Washington Jr' s roommate was an old friend who had attended Tuskegee, Juan E. Gomez. Booker T. Washington arranged this in the hope that Gomez, who was a good student, would have a good influence on his son, and

Booker T. Washington Jr. did well at Dummer. In 1907 both of them transferred to Phillips Exeter Academy, where Harlan P. Amen, the principal, was another admirer of Booker T. Washington. In the fall of 1908, however, Booker T. Washington Jr. suddenly left Exeter after refusing to be bound by its strict rules. The Exeter experience, however, shocked him into greater sobriety of behavior, and Booker T Washington later wrote a letter to Amen thanking him for bringing his son's life to a necessary crisis. Entering Fisk University, Booker T. Washington Jr. showed a new maturity of outlook, made good grades, edited the *Fisk Herald*, and graduated in 1913. Searching for a career, he vowed he would establish the largest Negro drugstore in the United States. In the fall of 1913 he enrolled in the Northwestern University School of Pharmacy.

On New Year's Eve 1913 he married Nettie Hancock, daughter of a teacher at Prairie View State College, herself a faculty member of the Colored Deaf, Dumb and Blind Institute in Austin, Texas. His wife accompanied him to Chicago for the rest of the school year, but in the summer of 1914 Booker T. Washington built the couple a house in Greenwood, the residential area for the Tuskegee faculty.

For the next four years Booker T. Washington Jr. worked for the Julius Rosenwald Foundation in its work of constructing rural black schoolhouses in the South. In 1918 he was appointed claims adjuster for the 9,000 black employees of the Muscle Shoals nitrate plant in northern Alabama. Lacking his father's tact, he made a speech that infuriated the local white people, who forced him to leave town.

He moved to Los Angeles, California, where he was a successful real-estate broker. His son Booker T. Washington III is an architect in New York City. His daughter Nettie married the grandson of Frederick Douglass.

R.L.H.

A Biographical Note on Ernest Davidson Washington

Ernest Davidson ('Dave') Washington (Feb. 6, 1889-1938), a son of Booker T. Washington and Olivia Davidson Washington, was a delicate child who shared his mother's physical infirmities as well as her gentle spirit and determination to struggle on. As befitted the youngest child, he was the most lovable. He attended the Tuskegee Institute training school. From the Spring of 1904 until December 1905 he attended Oberlin Academy, Oberlin, Ohio, where John Fisher Peck was principal. He boarded in town, and was only an average student. In 1905 he developed serious eye trouble that caused Booker T. Washington to consult the best eye physicians in New York and to withdraw his son from all close use of his eyes for about six months. The eye trouble continued throughout his life, but he graduated from Tuskegee and in 1910-11 studied at Talladega College in Alabama.

From the fall of 1911 to the spring of 1913 he attended Shaw University Medical School but failed to complete the course, possibly because of his eye trouble. Going to New York City, he enrolled in the New York School of Secretaries, taking stenography and typing, for which he had some background through earlier work in the Public Relations Department office at Tuskegee Institute. While there, he met and married Edith Merriweather, of an old Washington, D.C., family, a teacher in the Atlantic City, N.J., public schools. On the advice of his father, he continued his secretarial course through the remainder of the year, while his wife taught at the Childrens House at Tuskegee and made a closer acquaintance with her parents-in-law.

E. Davidson Washington served as northern financial agent of Tuskegee for many years, and for the last ten years of his life served the public relations office of Tuskegee Institute, guiding the thousands of visitors each year through the campus. He edited a compilation of the speeches of Booker T. Washington and a shorter volume of his quotations. He died after a year of failing health, apparently of heart trouble, as the age of forty-nine.[1]

---

[1] The announcement of the birth of Ernest Davidson Washington, February 6, 1889 and of a fire two days later that destroyed Booker T. Washington's house, appeared in the *Southern Workman*, 18 (Mar. 1889), 25.

R.L.H.

July 1883
To James Fowle Baldwin Marshall
Tuskegee, Alabama
July 23, 1883

Dear Gen'l: We thank you for extending the time on remainder due you on note.

I acknowledged the receipt of Mr. Carrington's money.

The basement is now being bricked up with brick from our first kiln. We were successful with the kiln though the work, by my absence, was not pushed as it should have been. It is hard to get a good foreman, one who will push hands and who also has a practical idea of all the details of the business. Shall try another man next time. The kiln contained about 70,000 brick and we have been lucky enough to sell them all except what we are using for the basement. Mr. Varner buys most of them. He will take now more than we have. Another kiln will be begun next week and I expect to see that the work is pushed. One of the merchants puts up a brick store soon as a result of the brick enterprise. It has done much good in many ways. I want to get hold of some letter files and a copying press. Will you be kind enough to advise as to the kind and where to get them.

I hope that Mr. Parrott is doing well. I sent you some papers containing accts. of our close. You will see that the South deals in high-sounding titles.

Yes, we have a sweet little girl which adds much to our happiness. With your permission Mrs. W. and I desire to call her "Portia Marshall Washington."
Sincerely yours,

B.T. Washington

A Biographical Note on James M. Poaches

James M. Poaches, who was my father's masseur, was also masseur for my stepmother Margaret who died in 1925.

The telephones were first installed in Tuskegee in 1895. The telephone system at Tuskegee Institute was donated by D.L. Carson, Southern Agent Bell Telephone Company.

My father suggested to Mrs. Mary Church Terrell that she get the Colored women together and form an organization. Mrs. Terrell and my step-mother Margaret were two of the first Presidents of the new organization. Mrs. Terrell had a strong influence among the women. She was well educated and came from Memphis, Tennessee, and went to Oberlin College to receive her education. She married a man who was a Judge and a great friend of my father. He was a Republican and often came and visited with my father. The families were very close. Mrs. Terrell died in 1954.

The last time that I saw Mrs. Terrell she was very old. Mrs. Terrell was the first Negro woman to serve on the Washington, D.C. Board of Education from 1895 to 1901 and then she served again from 1906 to 1911. Both periods were during my father's lifetime.

There was a very close relationship between the two families. Judge Terrell and James Cobb were members of what was called the

"Black Cabinet" during the term of President Theodore Roosevelt's office.*

Mrs. Terrell was the first President of the national Association of Colored Women's Groups.

Mrs. Terrell came to visit Tuskegee when my little brother Booker T. Washington, Jr. answered the door and Mrs. Terrell said: "I am Mrs. Mary Church Terrell." Brother said: "You're the lady Mom's always fussing about and talking about!"

President Roosevelt was genuinely fond of my father. He usually greeted him "I'm bully glad to see you, Mr. Washington". I came to the White House in 1908 with my father, husband, and little baby. The President gave me a bouquet of flowers and my husband a pin.

W. C. Handy, the writer of Beale Street Blues and St. Louis Blues was a great admirer of my father. He visited me on the 50th anniversary of Tuskegee Institute, which was about fourteen years after my father's death. Mr. Handy was a very modest man, quiet and unassuming. My father had no particular liking for Jazz. He preferred spirituals and hymns, particularly liked spirituals. "Turkey in the Straw" was a very favorite piece of my father's. My father took me to visit the widow of President Chester Arthur, Republican of Vermont, and left me there and I visited her for a week. President Arthur died in 1886. This was quite a while after his death. Mr. Arthur was living in Albany, N.Y. then.

My father loved to ride horseback. He rode until the time of his death. His horse was named Dexter. The horse had been named after a person rather than the street in Montgomery, Alabama.

I never visited Frederick Douglass' (1817-1895) home. But Frederick Douglass visited our home in Tuskegee. I remember sitting in his lap as a little girl. he came to our home to make a speech at one of the commencements. My father admired Frederick Douglass as much as any one individual. He got a lot of inspiration from him. Frederick Douglass was about 41 years older than my father. My step-mother Margaret James Murray was a classmate of Dr. W.E.B. Dubois- (1868-1963). There was no great difference in their age.

My father actually introduced to the public Dr. DuBois and Poet Paul Lawrence Dunbar (1872-1906) at the same time and on the same stage. My father knew that DuBois was an outstanding scholar, who was interested in everything and my father wanted him to teach at Tuskegee but DuBois refused.

---

* See pp. 134-136 for Portia's discussion of that term.

Misc. Notes:

Andrew Carnegie (1835-1919) Am. (Scot.-born) industrialist and Philanthropist

William McKinley (1843-1901) 25th Pres. (1897-1901)

Theodore Roosevelt (1858-1919) 26th Pres. (1901-1909)

William Howard Taft (1857-1930), 27th Pres. (1909-1913)

Mrs. Pittman visited for a week in the home of the widow of Pres. Chester Arthur, d. 1886, who was 21st Pres. (1881-1885)

Thomas Woodrow Wilson (1856-1924), 28th Pres. (1913-1921)

Grover Cleveland (1837-1908, 22nd Pres. (1885-89) and 1893-97).

P.M.W.P.

128

A Biographical Note on Jane Ethel Clark-Hill

*— Her spirit of unselfishness shall be an undying memory to
those who knew and loved her.*

Miss Jane Ethel Clark was the daughter of Mary Ethel and John
Clark. Miss Clark was born in Washington, D. C. April 24, 1878, but
moved to Newark, New Jersey at an early age. Portia Marshall Washington Pittman, daughter of Booker T. Washington, says: "My father
had a charming woman on the faculty by the name of Jane Ethel Clark, a
1901, Liberal Arts, (English) graduate of Oberlin College. Miss Clark
was my official chaperone in Europe. She was a gracious woman and
was called a raving beauty by European observers. We stopped in London and visited Samuel Coleridge-Taylor. He arranged for me 'Sometimes I Feel Like A Motherless Child.' When I arrived in Berlin, Germany, I played 'Sometimes I Feel Like A Motherless Child,' for Mr.
Martin Krause. When he asked me the question, What is that you are
playing? I replied, that is the music of my people." Miss Clark was also
the first Dean of Women at Tuskegee Institute. Mr. Washington often
stated that Miss Clark was very spiritual and musical and he wanted her
influence over the girls at Tuskegee. Later Miss Clark met at Tuskegee
Dr. Leslie Pinckney Hill. On June 29, 1907 in the Episcopal Church,

Newark, New Jersey, Jane Ethel Clark and Leslie Pinckney Hill were married. Mrs. Hill was the mother of six daughters: Eleanor Taylor Hill, Hermione Clark Hill, Elaine Serena Hill, Nathalie Du Bois Hill, Mary Dorothea Hill, and Emily Hildegarde Hill.

Mrs. Hill was a devoted wife and mother, setting the welfare of her husband above all responsibilities, and considering her highest accomplishment the healthy upbringing of her daughters to self-direction and self-support. In all this the unfailing strength of her deep religious convictions carried her triumphantly through all pain and sorrow. Her Church, with its Prayer Book and Hymnal, was the cornerstone of her faith and a constant consolation. She loved domesticated animals, garden plants, flowers, trees, and conscientiously fed whole companies of birds that flocked to the yard for the crumbs and seeds which she thought it her duty to supply. Mrs. Hill cared greatly for music and learning, and poetry and all gracious language. She never learned to answer ugly speech or spirit except by silence. Kindly humor was one of her healing resources. old and young alike, students, teachers, and neighbors felt the quiet dignity and calm of her presence and the warm sincerity of her friendship. In the last hours Jane Ethel Clark-Hill thought of the "Ten thousand times ten thousand in sparkling raiment bright," of "armies of the ransomed saints" thronging "the steeps of light," and of the golden gates flung wide to all who are victorious in the fight with death and sin and she said simply, "I think I shall be among them."

Author's Note: Mrs. Hill departed her life February 19, 1955 in the Woman's Medical College Hospital in Philadelphia, PA of heart ailment. Funeral Services, Calvary Episcopal Church, 814 North 41 Street, Philadelphia, Pennsylvania, 11:00 a.m., February 24, 1955. She is buried beside her daughter, Nurse Emily Hildegarde Hill, and her beloved husband, Dr. Leslie Pinckney Hill, in Union Hill Cemetery, Kennett Square, Pennsylvania.

R.N.H.

Letter of September 1884 from Olivia A. Davidson to Eleanor Jameson Williams Baker (Spruce Cottage Jackson, N.H. Sept. 6, 1884)

Dear Mrs. Baker,

I wish I could express to you my deep sense of all your kindness to me. I almost feel that it is an imposition, this having such long helpful letters from you in addition to all the arrangements and inquiries you are making for me.

Your letter came yesterday, and I did not reply in this morning's mail because I wished to take a night to think of it, and then it was too late to send to the mail. This is my reply to your proposition. I am willing to do anything that promises to restore me to health. If it were set for the uncertainty about what is the real state of my health, I should perhaps hesitate about going again to a hospital, but since the opportunity offers to assure myself whether or not there is internal trouble, I think it would not be wisdom to fail to benefit by it. My friends at Framingham are anxious to have me come there, and if it were not that 1 do not know what is the matter with me, and the fear that I might be losing time in trying to get well by resting only, I think I would prefer going there to going any place else as one, at least, of my best earthly

*friends is there (the one with whom I have been this summer, and who
has made me strong so often when I have grown discouraged). I was not
surprised to learn that Mrs. Hemenway offers me a home at Readville
for the present, as this is only in keeping with her great kindness
throughout. When I was at the hospital she came in person to tell me
that I need have no hesitancy in applying to her for whatever I needed.
If I were very, very rich in money, I could not repay Mrs. Hemenway all
I owe her, for whatever my life has been worth to me and to others in the
past few years is due to her. Through her the whole tenor of my life has
been changed. Thinking of all her kindness to me and all I owe to her I
have been unwilling to burden her so soon with my helplessness. Three
years was not long for one to work in a new field before completely
breaking down was it? But since before I was well grown I have had a
life, always full of work, and often full to overflowing of trouble and
suffering, so that when I went into the work at Tuskegee, though fresh
from school I was not fresh in bodily and mental strength.*

*It was a great surprise as well as pleasure to meet Gen.
Armstrong. He was not mistaken. I am trying to get the best out of my
stay here, and as far as possible, I refrain from thinking or worrying
about things, feeling willing to fold my hands and wait, if only in the end
I can be myself again and go back to work. It is pretty hard at times to
keep still and be patient and I could not do it alone, but I feel that my
Father is helping me, by surrounding me with as much that is beautiful
and lovely — Jackson grows more lovely every day — I think I would
never grow tired and sick if I could, when at work, drop all now and
then and go out and look at my beautiful mountains — "lift up mine eyes
to the hills — whence cometh my strength." I must not write more. If
Miss Jones has not gone please give her my best wishes for her success
in her new work. With best wishes for yourself and a deep sense of all
you have done and are doing for me, I am, Very truly yours*

Olivia A. Davidson

[1] Notes on follow-Up Discussion Between Portia Washington Pittman and Roy
Hill: Eleanor James Williams Baker (1885-91) was born in Boston. In 1840
she married Walter Baker of Dorchester, a manufacturer of chocolate and
cocoa, who left her a considerable fortune on his death in 1852. All of their
four children died in infancy. As a widow, Mrs. Baker devoted her considerable energies to a variety of charitable and intellectual pursuits, and
established a salon for Boston intellectuals. During the Civil War her house
was a center for making uniforms for the Massachusetts volunteer troops.
She was also active in hospital work for the wounded soldiers, and made

several tours of inspection of army hospitals. Among her efforts for the education of the blacks during Reconstruction and afterward was her provision of three annual scholarships at Hampton Institute after 1871. She also aided many individual blacks including Olivia A Davidson, who named her first child Baker T. Washington (later changed to Booker T. Washington, Jr.).

[2] That the letter was written in 1884 is shown by references in BTW to Samuel Chapman Armstrong, Sept. 11, 1884. (The letter is in the Library of Congress file: ALS Con. 949 BTW Papers DLC)

Portia T's Comments on the Term "The Black Cabinet"

The term Black Cabinet had long been a part of the jargon of Negro politicians. Originating during the period of Frederick Douglass's regime in Republican Party politics, the term had been applied consistently to whatever group of Negro leaders happened to be exercising some influence with the party in power in Washington, D.C. After 1895, for instance, Booker T. Washington and his Tuskegee machine constituted the Black Cabinet. James Weldon Johnson made this comment to my father during Theodore Roosevelt's administration:

"In Washington, I found myself a non-resident member of the "Black Cabinet." This was a group made up of colored men who held important federal positions in the capital. At the time, it included the Register of the Treasury, the Recorder of Deeds for the District, the Auditor of the Navy Department, an Assistant United States Attorney General, a Judge of the Municipal Court, and the Collector for the Port of Washington. . . . Those of the group who lived in Washington customarily met at lunch and discussed the political state of the nation, with special reference to its Negro citizens. On such matters, Booker T. Washington (my father) as chief adviser to President Roosevelt, and became the same to President Taft; but the "Black Cabinet" was not without considerable influence and power."

134

There was no such group during Woodrow Wilson's tenure in Washington.

The Black Cabinet of World War II included a few Negro political figures. Among its members, however, were such outstanding people as Walter White, of the NAACP; Lester Granger, of the Urban League; Channing Tobias, of the Young Men's Christian Association; Judge William H. Hastie; Mrs. Mary McLord Bethune; A. Philip Randolph, of the Union of Porters; and a score of lesser lights. No formal organization held the group together. Cooperation among them was purely voluntary, and it was motivated by their interest in the welfare of the race.

My step-mother Margaret Washington and Mary Church Terrell were always having their ups and downs about clubs and who was in charge. I grew to hate organizations. I just kept a watchful eye on the Black Cabinet of World War. II. The first Black Cabinet met so often in my home. My father would let his hair down and enjoy himself at the meetings in my home. He often said that I relaxed him.

The next movement that took a major stand in America was the movement started by Dr. Martin Luther King, Jr. That movement would have met with my father's approval. Dr. King's outlook was similar to my father's. Where Dr. King was an intellectual, my father was a practical man.

The Black Cabinet was very well known among the Negro masses, but every Negro who sought a well-paying position with the federal government soon knew that it was a power to be reckoned with. It was believed, although never entirely proved, that all significant Negro appointments were first cleared through this group.

To ascertain the Negro's honest opinions and feelings toward my father would be a difficult task. For racial antagonism in the South, as well as a thinly veiled hostility to the Negro, had made the Negro a reticent individual. Apparently, however, Washington had an immense popularity among Southern Negroes. Booker T. Washington Clubs were established in all parts of the South, and there was hardly a Negro home without a picture of the new Black leader adorning its walls. But educated Negroes examined Washington's career with a deeper insight. One of them thus summed up the reasons for Booker 'T's fame with the race:

Mr. Washington's following was at first very largely prudential and constrained; it lacked spontaneousness and joyance. He was not hailed with glad acclaim as the deliverer of his people. He brought good gifts rather than glad tidings. Many believed in him for his work's sake; some acquiesced rather than antagonize one who had gained so large a measure of public confidence; others were willing to co-operate in the accomplishments of good deeds, though they inwardly detested his doctrine; while those of a political instinct sought his favor as a pass key to prestige and place.

Biographical Sketch On Portia T's Best Friend and Fellow-Musician: Hazel Lucile Harrison, May 12, 1883-April 28, 1969

Hazel Harrison, American concert pianist, was born in La Port, Ind., the only child of Hiram and Olive Jane (Woods) Harrison. Her parents were direct descendants of pioneering black people who had fled the slave system in southern states and followed legendary escape routes to the midwestern United States and southern Ontario. Olive Harrison, who had been born in Canada, was a hairdresser and manicurist whose customers came from La Porte's most prominent families. Hiram Harrison, born in Michigan, worked as a laborer and rural postman and was, by 1884, co-proprietor of Stevesand and Harrison, a barber shop close to the central business district of La Porte. He had a beautiful tenor voice, sang with the choir of the Central Presbyterian Church, and was organizer, director, and accompanist of its Sunday school choir.

Hazel Harrison's exceptional talents, manifest at an early age, were fostered by her father. She began piano lessons at four with Richard Pellow, an accomplished English organist and choirmaster of the Harrison's church. By age eight Hazel was supplementing the family income by playing for dancing parties. At one such party, according to

La Porte legend, a distinguished German musician, Victor Heinze, heard her and offered to become her teacher.

Heinze's tutelage and influence were major factors in Hazel Harrison's development as a pianist. Through her study with him, she acquired a remarkable keyboard technique, a lyrical quality of playing, and a large repertory. She remained his student for many years, commuting to Chicago when Heinze moved all his teaching activity there from La Porte. In Chicago, devoted and knowledgeable patrons of music praised her as Heinze's most accomplished student; encouragement also came from prominent members of the city's black community.

In 1902, Hazel Harrison graduated from La Porte High School. She remained at home, intensifying preparations for a career as a concert pianist and teaching music to the children of La Porte's leading families. The trips to Chicago for lessons continued, as did employment as a dance pianist in both cities.

The horizons of Harrison's career widened when in the spring of 1904 she received an invitation to appear as soloist with the Berlin Philharmonic Orchestra under August Scharrer. The concert took place on October 22 at the Berlin Singacademie; she performed two concerti, the A minor by Grieg and the E minor of Chopin. It was the first appearance with an orchestra in Europe of an American artist whose entire musical education had taken place on home soil. Berlin critics were unanimous in praise: she was described as a "musical wonder," a "sensation," and a "virtuoso."

She returned at once to La Porte, resuming the cycle of teaching, studying, and performing. A recital at Kimball Hall in Chicago in 1910 brought critical acclaim and an appeal from a veteran musical critic for financial assistance to enable her to return to Germany for further study. Response came from two Chicago music philanthropists and Harrison began lessons early in 1911 in Berlin with Hugo van Dalan. He arranged an audition for her with Ferruccio Busoni, the world-renowned Italian pianist and composer. Busoni responded to the "strength, rhythm, and poetry" of the young pianist and agreed to supervise her training, reversing his earlier decision not to accept new pupils.

Hazel Harrison was drawn immediately into the closely knit circle in Berlin of the Busoni family, pupils, and intimate associates, and a close bond was established between teacher and student. She embraced the unique Busonian precepts and dicta: recognition of similitudes among the arts, musical eclecticism, program-building on the grand scale, and recognition of the sonorities of the piano as echoing those of orchestral sound. Busoni exhorted the young artist to visit art galleries, to study German philosophy and folk literature, to engage in ensemble playing, and to "live more . . . all will show in your playing." During Busoni's absences from Berlin, Harrison worked on keyboard technique with his young protegé and assistant, the Dutch pianist Egon Petri.

This remarkable experience ended in 1914 with the outbreak of World War I. Hazel Harrison returned to the United States and moved from La Porte to Chicago. She was joined there by her mother in 1920 and shortly thereafter by Hiram Harrison who had been separated from the family for many years. On Sept. 1, 1919, she married Walter Bainter Anderson, a beauty products manufacturer and salesman; the marriage ended in divorce in the late 1920s.

Hazel Harrison's fame as a pianist grew to considerable proportions during the 1920s, as recital tours under various managements took her many times across the country. In 1927 she returned to Germany to study for a brief period with Petri. The depression years took their toll, however, forcing her into an expanded teaching career but in no way causing her to abandon her efforts as a concert artist. She worked indefatigably on enlarging a repertory recognized for its brilliance and technical difficulty. Harrison was an early proponent of comtemporary composers of the Soviet Union, Poland, and Germany and of "synesthesia," the association of color and sound on a systematic and consistent basis. Her programs included compositions of polysensory intent by Alexander Scriabin and Alexander Laszlo and unpublished works by black composers of her acquaintance as well as the more familiar but stunning variations and fantasies built on the waltzes of Johann Strauss and the transcriptions for piano of organ works of Bach written by Liszt and by Busoni.

Recitals at Aeolian and Town Halls in New York City, at Jordan Hall in Boston, at Kimball Hall in Chicago, and in major American and Canadian musical centers brought Harrison continued praise. In 1940 Glenn Dillard Gunn, music critic of the Washington (D.C.) Times Herald, wrote: "She has today a technical equipment that is definitely that of a virtuoso, and her gift for pianistic address is vivid, urgent and eloquent." Nonetheless, access to the mainstream of the concert business in the United States — annual performances in the great concert halls, appearances with major symphony orchestras, and contracts with the important recording companies — was denied her because of her race. The 1904 Berlin engagement was Hazel Harrison's only appearance as soloist with a major symphony orchestra during its normal concert season. She played with the Minneapolis Symphony under Eugene Ormandy in 1932 in a concert at the Tuskegee (Ala.) Institute, and with the Hollywood Bowl Symphony under Zeler Solomon in August 1949 during a convention of the National Association of Negro Musicians, both appearances under special circumstances and before special audiences.

An enthusiastic review of a 1922 Chicago recital had ended in a somber prophetic vein: "She is extremely talented...it seems too bad that the fact that she is a Negress may limit her future plans." The pattern of segregated audiences and management systems characterizing the business of concert performance of the day yielded rarely to include this exceptional artist and her audiences remained largely those of her own race. She gained an enormous following throughout the United States, however, and was the unrivaled pianist of the day for the nation's black music lovers.

Hazel Harrison's accomplishments as a teacher of piano are also of great significance. During a long and distinguished teaching career she was instrumental in developing a number of outstanding younger musicians. In November 1931, Harrison had joined the faculty of the School of Music at Tuskegee Institute, newly organized by her friend William Dawson, noted composer and choir director. Leaving Tuskegee in 1937, she became head of the piano faculty at Howard University in Washington, D.C. She also taught for brief periods at Alabama State College in Montgomery and at Jackson College in Mississippi. In 1945 she established at Howard the Olive J. Harrison Piano Scholarship Fund in memory of her mother. Subsequent annual recitals by her students and her own appearances served as benefits for the fund. During the 1940s and 1950s she also gave benefit recitals for war relief and for partisan causes sponsored by groups sympathetic to civil uprisings in the Soviet Union, Spain, and Latin America. On leave from Howard from 1947 to 1950 she toured the United States, and in 1952 the western provinces of Canada.

For a short period during the 1950s Harrison was married to Allen Moton, an Alabama businessman and a friend of long standing. me marriage ended in divorce. She resigned from Howard in 1957 and move to New York City. In 1965 she went south, to La Grange, Ga., and Montgomery, Ala., seeking a gentler climate. Returning to Washington, D.C., she lived in the home of a former student, the Reverend Alphonso Harrod, and then in the nursing home where she died in 1969 of congestive heart failure. During her last years, she became immersed in reading philosophy. She had continued as long as possible to teach, practiced daily, and played for small groups of friends in the Harrod home.

[Correspondence between Harrison and members of the Harreld

family from 1903 to 1965, clippings, photographs, and recital programs are held by Josephine Harreld Love. There is also some material in the Moorland-Springarn Coll., Howard Univ. Her career may be traced in the files of the La Porte, Ind., Daily Record and Argus Bulletin, and the Chicago Tribune, Inter-Ocean, and Record-Herald. Family information was verified through municipal and county records in La Porte. Published biographical information and commentary is scanty; see Maude Cuney Hare, Negro Musicians and Their Music (1936); "Men of the Month," in The Crisis, Dec. 1912; and a tribute to her in an article by Ralph Ellison, her student at Tuskegee, "The Little Man at Chehaw Station: The American Artist and His Audience," American Scholar, Winter 1978-79. Assistance was provided by William Dawson of Tuskegee; by Florence Andrew, Rev. John Deason, and Ruth Tallant, all of La Porte; and by Catherine Moton Patterson, Portia Trenholm Jenifer, Doris McGinty, Benjamin Ward, Rev. Alphonso Harrod, and Vivian Scott. A death certificate was obtained from the D.C., Dept. of Health.]

R.L.H.

NOTABLE AMERICAN WOMEN, The Modern Period; A Biographical Dictionary, by Josephine Harreld Love, 1980, pp 317-319.

Eulogy Delivered at Obsequies for Portia Marshall Washington Pittman

(Daughter of the Honorable Booker T. Washington, Tuskegee Institute, Alabama)

The time and the place of a woman's life on the earth is the time and the place of her body, but the meaning, the significance of her life is as far reaching and redemptive as her gifts, her dedication, her response to the demands of her time and the total commitment of her powers can make it.. Portia Pittman is dead. This is her fact and our reality. To those who are a part of her by ties of blood and intimacy we hesitate to profane your sorrow with our spoken words. Out of our own sorrow, though detached, we share with you the agony of your grief. The anguish of your heart finds echo in our own. We cannot enter into all you feel or,bear with you the burden of your pain, but from within the privacy of our own spirits we give the strength of our caring, the warmth of those who seek to understand the silent, storm-swept barrenness of so great a loss. And, we do this, each of us, in quiet ways so that on your loneliest task you will not have to walk alone.

It is my assignment to speak of the present as the living experience of a living woman, Portia Pittman. Obviously, this cannot be done. But, what one may do is to feel somewhat of the texture and the fabric of this gifted woman. To her the present was the point at which the past and the future meet. She saw more clearly than most others that the present was always becoming the past and the future was always becoming the present. Hence, there was in the present much to determine the past as a goodly heritage and to shape the future as a fulfillment of our dreams and hopes. What of the present? It is at least a time of paradox and dilemma. The paradox in all of this is that American life is largely controlled and dominated by white society. Within that society there is a minority who have in their hands the power of the veto and certification over the economic and, in some ways, the social life of the vast majority of the population, both black and white, while at the same time this vast majority is poor and dependent. That such contrasts exist and persist in our society is the essence of a most cruel paradox. Portia Marshall Washington Pittman understood this as few women do in our time. Her commitment was two-fold. One, to the-overwhelming task of feeling her way into the grain in the wood of the dominant society and to rationalize that insight in the development of techniques of understanding and negotiation. This understanding made her aware of the areas of vulnerability in which a social conscience could be aroused and evoked, while the negotiation would emanate from within a common framework of enlightened self-interest. Mrs. Pittman knew no matter how far ahead of itself a turtle puts its two front feet, it cannot move its body until it brings up its hind legs. Simple, but nevertheless profound, insights such as this informed all of her negotiations, strategies and planning.

The second aspect of her commitment was to the masses of the poor. It was her insight that the black poor are not only poor but they also live in an intimate climate of poverty. The climate of poverty is an inter-atmosphere of the spirit. It dries up the springs of one's self-esteem and often renders impotent one's confidence in the meaning and the significance of one's life. She identified with the plight of the poor, and in so doing placed her professional skills and the resources of her work at their disposal. But she did more than this. She identified with the poor woman and man herself. It was this latter identification that made heavy her days and placed at the center of her spirit an unrelieved frustration. Thus, she could empathize with the fear, the despair, the anger, and the stark lives of those who had no wind break of economic security behind which they could take refuge and give to their families some measure of immunity against the impersonal economic forces surrounding their lives!

She worked with this paradox throughout her professional life, constantly seeking to create ways by which the poor would be brought into direct contact with the resources of the rich, thereby creating a community of common sharing, mutual dependence, and effective economic participation. She was a bridge between them but she was not a beggar. Instinctively she seemed to have known how hard it is for one person to forgive another person because he is able to help him.

Thus, her creative genius expressed itself in recognizing the healthy self-respect that accrued to the man who was able to exchange his skill in the open market for goods, services, and security. Such is the paradox. In thinking about the greatness of Portia Pittman one is often reminded of the problems faced by public figures who are dealing on their own terms, and in their own ways with the great issues that beset the times in which they lived. How often they are misunderstood and as a result of this subjected to a caustic and unjustified criticism. Their best efforts are directed to the task of coming to grips with the real world as it is. To perceive it properly, is to understand it and to contribute to the alteration of it in ways that lend themselves to the humanizing and civilizing task of man's experience. As they proceed to pursue this great mission which their vision of great society has stimulated them to do they often find themselves under attack by radicals for being too docile and passive and similarly from conservatives for being too aggressive and militant. Yet they proceed and in so doing they manifest the substance and compassion which is within them.

I allow myself only a summarizing comment on one of the central dilemmas of the present. Mrs. Pittman recognized the new sense of positive identity which was evolving in the black community growing out of the demand for separateness in contrast with the desire to establish a sense of community with the larger white society. She saw clearly that a man must be at home somewhere before he can be at home everywhere. She was a black woman and identified her roots with her own people. It was her understanding that in the perspective of history the will to separate and the will to segregate often could not be distinguished from each other. Yet there is a difference. For most of her life Portia Pittman lived and experienced an America which imposed segregation, "apartness", on the masses of black citizens. This new thrust which embodies a voluntary expression of some black people is fundamentally different from the segregation era.

Yet because her life span transcended such a significant period of the modern black people's experience she had little difficulty differentiating between the two orientations and understanding they were based upon. Because of her insight and wisdom gained over long years of involvement with the struggles of her people, Portia Pittman clearly understood that between black and white America, there must always be a swinging door which no man and no circumstance must be allowed to shut. To our dear sister Portia, ours is a common destiny. Therefore, she put the weight of her mind, the gift of her imagination, and the magic of her humor on the side of a concept of society big enough to provide for the widest divergence, to nourish each other in a creative continuum of fulfillment which was to her the genius of the democratic creed. Thus, we celebrate her life and thank God for the gift that permitted her to companion our days. The time and the place of this woman's life on the earth is as far reaching and redemptive as her gifts, her dedication, her response to the demands of God's time, and the total commitment of her powers can make it.

Roy L. Hill

Dream Prologue

A very different woman from Portia Pittman is extolled in "A Birthday Tribute". Many streams united to form the stream of life that was Nettie Douglass. A granddaughter of the redoubtable Booker T. Washington, she joined her life to that of Frederick Douglas III, a grandson of the formidable Frederick. From such roots, what splendid fruit! Here was a woman FREE TO BE, long before those words became clichéd. To her, all things belonged and she reached out slim brown fingers to every aspect of her heritage. She never scorned the lowly, she embraced the blues, she conquered the big time, all in one passionate while of living. Here is a role model for young black women who refuses imitation and demands of each young woman a UNIQUE expression of a priceless inheritance.

Looking good, she was dancing to Lord Keep Me From Sinking Down. "I'm not impressed. I'm relieved and he's gone." Echoes from a low down time behind the monument.
Can't love me? — Leave me! Seem right to me, you can know me. Diamonds have always been my best friends. Love, leave, love, love. Wait a minute. Get this beat! I am the Duke of Ellington; the King of Cole; the Count of Basie;

and a Queen I'm told. That's how Stella Voorhees got her man. Les McCann. "I've been down-so long that down don't worry me no mo'." Sly and that low life cow O, be what you are. What goes around also comes around too. Go long child! I've been lonely too long.

The sun is shining for her people now. My, my, the soup line. A chicken in every pot. The welfare girls on relief being relieved. He's gone. Carry a big stick and walk hard, work hard. No tip, Baby. Now tip, Baby. Hello Dixiana, Alabama. Love is a religious experience. Might as well be! Whose life is it? It's mine. Lonely, leave, love will make you drink and gamble make you — love! — do what you know is wrong. Dance goodlooking love girl, strange girl!

She is strange, so are the plays of Strindberg, Tennessee Williams, Ed Bullins, Alice Childress and James Baldwin. She is far-out, and at the same time common. So are raw eggs in South Carolina and Ted Shine's "Contribution." She is different. So was St. Sebastian, Josephine Baker, James Brown and Joan of Ark. So is Bea Richards. So is Hazel Scott. She is a club member, a colored girl, an Afro-American, a homey from Down Home, Tuskegee, Alabama. She went to California and hit the Big Towns the big towns, the Jet Set, the Nat King Coles, the Josephine Bakers and she is still from down home. She did it mostly all by herself. Her name is Nettie Hancock Washington Douglass.

She was born hip. Her mother's mother was a hip mother and her father's grandmother was a mighty mother. Maybe that's why the Nettie Blues. But she's one of the Washington women, first. Autumn Allegro. She loves swimming in the Pacific Ocean and when the spirit leaves her well-preserved body, I hear she'll sign it over to the George Washington Carver University for the education of Science students.

She has a flair, but no air. She has class, but does not wear it on her shoulders. Only chips. She is unique. You either like her or you don't. If you don't, you won't, if you do—wheee—ouuu-eu! You do! Some folks never did learn to like Lillian Smith's *Strange Fruit*. Some folks don't like Booker T. Washington. And some people are bemused by the great Frederick Douglass. To some Josephine Baker never meant peanuts. To others Lead Belly could come for free and Jackie Robinson is not worth a dime. Roy Campanella maybe drug your Mama and Moms Mabley your Papa. Tastes differ; for some tastes Ethel Waters, *His Eye Is On The Sparrow* was and Bill Robinson is, Sugar Ray Robinson was and Joe Lewis is, Jack Johnson was and Eartha Kitt is.

But Fats Waller, no! Lucky Millender, no! Lil Green, no! Billie Holiday, never! And don't mention Blanche or Cab Calloway.

Everybody has a right to like whoever he is; and whatever he likes in life and in the arts. Some folks in religion like the Rev. Ike, some like Prophet Jones, others prefer Father Divine and some the Rt. Rev. Lawrence Thurgood. In literature many read Leopold Senghor and some read Imamu Amiri Baraka. In politics, some like Maynard Jackson and some like the Rev. Jesse Jackson. In food, some like chitterlings, some caviar. In entertainment, some like Aretha Franklin, some like Roberta Flack, some like the Ink Spots, and some like Bobby Blue Bland. Why should anyone like her—because she is a social worker, psychologist, housewife and lover of the finer things of life. She works well, well, simply well, complicatedly well, theatrically well, dramatically well, madly well, not just well.

She went to the Supreme Court, emotionally, to stop *Booker T's Child* from being published. Was she unaware of the rip-off white writers are doing, have been doing, to part of her own heritage.

When she walks, men gaze from afar. In her dancing, one sees her culture and that she can take and destroy. Drink like you live dirty Dan! Where would you be in life without Nettie? Off the street and onto the avenue of life. No man ever crosses her path who can't be governed by a clock: 8 hours on the job and the rest belongs to her! You see, her real friends can work shifts: one for the two of them; the second shift devoted to writing Poems and Plays about her. The third shift, they get high and sleep for hours, wake up and go to work and start all over again. The worldrunners are serious about maintaining control but Nettie says, "Honey, don't think about getting others together, if you ain't got no soul."

She has been up and down because of a California con-artist. She is much together now. Living her social scene in Mary-land beyond the district line.

Why should one like Nettie?—because she sings a song differently? Plenty Social Worker singers sing songs differently. Others strain hard to be different, but with no conviction. And some pay arrangers money to make them different. Some seem hollow, artificial, fake, and wrong when they sing a song. Nettie is as different as beer is from *champagne*; crackers from crepes suzettes; Governor George Wallace from Leroi Jones; Dallas, Texas from Paris, France —each real in their way, but Oh! how different and how fake it is if it is not real. You want the "City of Light!"

The letters L I V E that spell live mean exactly the same as the letters N E T T I E that spell Nettie. As for the work Douglass—be cool, JOHN be cool! And listen to N E T T I E.

Dramatic Epilogue

Live, NETTIE, Live
Live!
Unsinkable, unflappable
NETTIE!
She sings, plays the piano and dances.

Like Ertha Kitt is, she is a complex individual who likes "pretty music," "guys," caviar, good wine—the elegant life. She can *cock* an *eyebrow* and, green eyes communicating and comprehending, dip a shoulder, snapping a finger in time to "Do Nothing 'Till you Hear From Me." Right on, John. John John, Tell her again John that you want to be her pride and joy although she's been around the world and has honors and degrees hanging on her basement wall, Fats Waller doesn't want her to be too renowned. That perfect dresser with an air of good humor. "All the sad young men?" "No"—*Tender Is the Night.* Or Billy Budd on a cool evening. You don't have anything forever.

R.N.H.

Eulogy for Nettie Douglass

To our dear Sister Nettie Hancock Washington Douglass, ours is a common destiny. Therefore, she put the weight of mind, the gift of her imagination, and the magic of her humor on the side of the concept of society big enough to provide for the widest divergence, to nourish each other in a creative continuum of fulfillment which was to her the genius of the democratic creed. Thus, we celebrate her life and thank God for the gift that permitted her to companion our days. The time and the place of this woman's life on the earth are as far reaching and redemptive as her gifts, her dedication, her response to the demands of God's time, and the total commitment of the powers that were hers.

> Then the ebony bird beguiling,
> My sad face from smiling,
> While some nodded, almost napping, gently tapping and rapping,
> To the glow that was,
> They classic face that was,
> I stood there wondering, fearing,
> Doubting, hoping and dreaming dreams not dared to dream before,
> And the only word there spoken
> Was a whispered word.

Frederick Douglass the third and Nettie Washington the second
met socially in New York.
But their love was stronger than the love of those who
Were older, wiser than they.
And the stars never rose
Without Nettie's smile.
What an astonishing, ascending personality was
This Nettie the second.

This I whispered, and an echo murmured back the words:
Booker the third, Larry, Kenneth and Kenneth, Nettie the third,
Douglass Washington, Nettie the fourth and Fannie H. Douglass.

Back into the house on Massachusetts Avenue,
Living her social scene in Maryland beyond the district line,
Unsinkable, unflappable Nettie the second.

In the evening on Massachusetts Avenue
Such a gathering of professional friends you could meet.
Hear great Langston Hughes, and Gwendolyn Brooks' verse,
Greet a universal man or woman,
Or Plato's dialogue rehearse.
That Socrates with his last breath
Sublimely said of life and death.
Classical music,
Good wine,
O' the elegant life!

All my soul within me turning,
Soon I heard again a calling
Somewhat louder than before.
Surely I said, surely there are,
Louise, Margaret, Edith and Gloria at my window.
Let me see, she smiled and said,
What a treat this is!
Let my heart be still a moment To hear discourse so plainly.
Her many friends sitting lonely
Spoke only with a silent nod.
She loved with a love that was more than love.
The complex historical lady now at rest.

151

So with comprehending eyes and quick surmise,
And that each day was like a year.
A year whose days are long,
We watched her day by day
And wondered if each one of us
Would end the self-same way.
Like two doomed ships that pass in storm
We had crossed each other's way
But we made no sign, we said no word,
We had no word to say.

And though I was a soul in pain
My pain I could not feel.
She looked upon the garish day
With such wistful eye,
At that little tent of blue
Which friends called the sky.

Blest were the wrecked, the shocked, the seized,
The mutilated, the diseased
Who came to thee, for all were eased.
All those majestic traits
Told always of an inward grace.

And all they charm of mind and heart
And loveliness became a part
Of God's immortal healing art.

For Oak and Elm have pleasant leaves —
Her last look at the sky.
It is sweet to dance to violins
When love and life are fair.
To dance to flutes,
To dance to lutes is delicate and rare.
But it is just as sweet with nimble feet
To dance upon the air.
And then August the seventh
The Sun fell out of the sky.
The magic of our beloved Nettie the second has slipped into the air.

Epilogue

She had gone, but she shall be remembered with the lives
grown out of her life, the lives flashing her dream of the
beautiful culture, a needful thing.

After the cloud embankments,
The lamentation of wind,
I sighed for the new revelation,
And waited for miracles to rise
And tired moments wait, courage gone, and
Yet to win from Time and Death a moment's grace.
O, Nettie, precious Nettie, the memories are all in our minds now.

R.N.H.

SOME BOOKS AND PAMPHLETS ABOUT BOOKER T. WASHINGTON

Bacon, Alice Mabel. The Negro and the Atlanta Exposition, 1896.

Boone, Theodore Sylvester. The Philosophy of Booker T. Washington, the Apostle of Progress, the Pioneer of the New Deal, 1939.

Drinker, Frederick E. Booker T. Washington, the Master Mind of a Child of Slavery, 1915.

Fauset, Arthur Huff. Booker T. Washington, 1924.

Hubbard, Elbert. Little Journeys to the Homes of Great Teachers, 1908.

Jackson, Walter Clinton. A Boy's Life of Booker T. Washington, 1922.

Jones, W. M. A. A Fight for Education, the Story of Booker T. Washington's Earlier Days Related and Simplified with Questions, 1939.

Mathews, Basil Joseph. Booker T. Washington, Educator and Interracial Interpreter, 1948.

Matthews, Victoria E. Black-belt Diamonds: Gems from the Speeches, Addresses, and Talks to Students of Booker T. Washington, 1898.

Miller, Kelly. Booker T. Washington Five Years After, 1921

The Negro Problem; A Series of Articles by Representative American Negroes Today, 1903.

Pike, Godfrey Holden. From Slave to College President; being the Life Story of Booker Taliaferro Washington, 1902.

Riley, Benjamin Franklin. The Life and Times of Booker T. Washington, 1916.

Scott, Emmett Jay. Booker T. Washington, Builder of a Civilization, 1916.

Shaw, John W. A Tangled Skein: A Vindication of Booker T. Washington and His Work, 1904.

Spencer, Samuel R., Jr. Booker T. Washington and the Negro's Place in American Life, 1955.

Stevenson, Augusta. Booker T. Washington, Ambitious Boy, 1950

Stokes, Anson Phelps. A Brief Biography of Booker T. Washington, 1936.

Thrasher, Max Bennett. Tuskegee: Its Story and Its Work, 1900.

U. S. Congress. House. Committee on Coinage, Weights and Measures. Commemorative Coins, Booker T. Washington Commemorative Coin, 1946.

Washington, E. Davidson (Compiler). Quotations of Booker T. Washington, 1938.

Washington, E. Davidson (Editor). Selected Speeches of Booker T. Washington, 1932.

Great Lives Observed, Booker T. Washington, Edited by Emma Lou Thornbrough. Copyright 1969 by Prentice-Hall, Inc.

Booker T. Washington and His Critics. Problems in American Civilization. Edited with an introduction by Hugh Hawkins, D.C. Heath and Company, Copyright, 1962.

Negro Thought in America: 1880-1915. (Racial Idelogies in the Age of Booker T. Washington) by August Meier, The University of Michigan Press, 1969.

Booker T. Washington, The Making of a Black Leader: 1856-1901, by
Louis R. Harlan. New York Oxford University Press, 1972.
The Booker T. Washington Papers Volume 1. The autobiographical
writings. Editor Louis R. Harlan. University of Illinois Press.
Urbana, 1972.
The Booker T. Washington Papers Volume 2, 1860-1889. University of
Illinois Press. Editor Louis R. Harlan, Urbana, 1972.
The Booker T. Washington Papers Volume 3. University of Illinois
Press. Editor Louis R. Harlan, Urbana, 1973.

Left to Right-John H. Washington, Edith Olivia Washington, Mrs. Nettie Han-
cock Washington (Mrs. Booker T. Washington II), Booker T. Washington III,
Nettie Hancock Washington-Douglass, Frederick Douglass III (great-grandson of
Frederick Douglass), Lilla Washington and Gloria Davidson Washington.

A/Left to Right-Kenneth Morris, Nettie Douglass Washington, IV., Mayor Thomas Bradley (Mayor of Los Angeles, CA), Nettie, III., Kenneth Washington, Sr., all grandchildren of Nettie Hancock Washington Douglass and Dr. Frederick Douglass III. B/Left to Right-Hattie McDaniel, Mrs. Pittman, Walter Huston, Fannie Pittman and Mercedes McCambridge.

A

B

A/Portia, Booker T. Jr., and Margaret; back row, Booker T., II and E. Davidson Washington at their summer home in Hunnington, Long Island. B/The descendents of Booker T. at Tuskegee's 50th celebration: front row, Left to Right-Gloria Washington, Louise Washington, Edith Washington, Margaret Washington; second row, Left to Right-Edith Mae kelley Johnston, James Burroughs Washington Booker T.'s brother), Mrs. Susan Washington (Mrs. John H. Washington), Ed. Davidson Washington, Portia, George Washington Johnstone (Amanda's son), Hattie Calloway Washington (James Washington's wife); back row, Left to Right-Lilla Washington, Margaret Washington Barringtons, John Barrington, Fannie Pittman, Edith Merriweather Washington.

159

Index

Frances Hughes 4
Franklin, Benjamin 84
Fred A. Seaton 89
Friesland 44

G

Gautier, W.J. 8
Germania 45
Giants (then of New York City) 93
Gibson, Charles Dana 23
Gibson girl 23
Gloria 85
Goodall, Ted 3
Graduate School Chronicle 99
Grainger, Percy 75
Grambling College xi
Grant, Ulysses (President) 84
Great War 66
Green, C.W. 31
Greta Gandy 2
Grieg 47
Griffin, W.R. 53

H

Hackley, Azalea 57
Hale's Ford 9
Hall of Fame 85
Hall of Fame for Great Americans 84
Hampton Institute 7, 8, 13 85
Hampton University 68
Handy, W.C 74
Harlan, Louis 98
Harrison, Hazel xiii, 75, 76, 80, 94
Hart 33
Hart, Mabel I. 42
Hatcher family 10
Hawthorne, Nathaniel 84
Hayes, Rutherford B. (Mrs.) (Lemonade Lucy) 13
Hazel Gray 3
Heinrich, Albert Wilhelm (of the House of Hohenzollern) 43
Hemenway, Mary 17
Hemenway, Mary Tilesteon 13
Hill, Roy L. 95
Hillis, Newell (Reverend) 43
Hines, Earl 67

Hiram Davidson 21
Hoffman, Josef 47
Hohenlohe, Chlodwig (Prince) 46
Hortense Taylor 4
Howard University 70, 80
Howard University Chapel 94
Hughes, Langston 3
Hunt, Nathan 53

I

Invisible Man 99
Irma 3
Irving, Washington 64, 84

J

Javits, Jacob 87
Jay 3
Jazz Age 70
Jefferson, Thomas (President) 84
"Jim Crow" 87
John Washington 24
Johnson, Buddy 67, 69
Johnson, Charles L. 3
Johnson, J. Rosamond 68
Johnson, Jack (the "Great White Hope") 65
Johnston, G.W.A. 53
Joseph Davidson 12
Julliard School of Music 76

K

Kansas City Wranglers 3
Karrer, Eva Salome 42
Katzenbach, Nicholas 92
Kennedy, Alonzo Marcelle 89, 90, 93
Kennedy, J.A. xiv
Kennedy, Phala xiv
Kennedys 92
Kenny, John A. 62
King, Dora S. 21, 22
King, Martin Luther, Jr. xvi, 93
Kingfish Lewis 2
Knights of Pythias 58
Knotts, Louise A. 42
Krause, Martin 45, 46, 47, 53
Ku Klux Klan 12

L

Lane, Allen 82
Langston University 68
Lanier, Sidney 84
Lawrence, William (Bishop) 31
Lee, Eddie 3
Lee, Jenny 74
Lee, Robert E. 84
Leelu McDaniel 4
Lincoln, Abraham (President) 84
Liszt 45
Liszt Society 45
Little, A.H. (Reverend) 43
Living Good Franklin (Jim) 2
Lloyd's *Register of Ships* 81
Lois Lewis 3
Long, Carrie 3
Longview, Sara Lou 2
Longworth, Alice Roosevelt ("Miss Alice") 44, 94
Louise 82
Loulee Walton 3
Lucius D. Clay (General) 94
Lusitania 61

M

MacCracken, Henry M. 84
Macedonia Baptist Church 59
Madame Selicka 34
Malcolm X xvi
Mamie Jones 3
Manassas School 45
Mann, Thomas 50
Margaret J. Murray Washington 23-28, 30, 31, 35, 39, 44, 50, 51, 54
Marshall, James Fowler Baldwin (General) 8
Martha Jean 3
Mary Lou Pegues 4
Massachusetts General Hospital 18
Massachusetts Institute of Technology 5, 49
McDougall (Professor) 39
McDuffie, (Mrs.) 73
McKinley, William (President) xvi, 43
Meredith, James 92

Metropolitan Church 57
Millinder, Lucky 79
Mitchell, Abby (or Abbie) xiii, 47, 75
Mitchell, Leonard 77
Moore, Mary C. 24, 31, 32, 36
Morse, Samuel F.B. 84
Moton, Robert Russa 54, 73, 75
Mount Alto Vetran's Hopsital 93
Mozart 34
"Mr. Poaches" 62, 63
Mulzac, Hugh (Captain) 82
Murray, James 23
Murray, Lucy 23

N

NAACP 100, 101
National Association of Coloured Women 73
National Educational Association 67
National Youth Administration 82
New England General Hospital 16
New York Age 52, 55
New York Evening Sun 40
New York Times 81, 82
New York University's Gould Memorial Library 85
Niagara Movement 100
Nixon, Richard (President) 94

O

Oberlin Academy 55
Oberlin College 22
"Old Miss" 93
Oliver McPherson 4
Oliver, Robert T. xi

P

Paderewski, Ignace Jan 32
Paine, Tom 84
Palmer, Alice Freeman 42
Paul 3
Paula Wallace 2
Peabody, Annie Louise 42, 44, 45
Pearl James 3
Pee Wee Jones 2
Pennsylvania State University xi